hampsteadtheatre presents

in the club

by Richard Bean

hampsteadtheatre gratefully acknowledges the support of

hampsteadtheatre presents

In The Club
by Richard Bean

Cast (in alphabetical order)

Sasha	**Sian Brooke**
Gendarme	**Dermot Canavan**
Philip Wardrobe	**James Fleet**
Beatrice Renard	**Anna Francolini**
Andre	**Huw Higginson**
Frau Flugelhammerlein	**Carol Macready**
Nicola Daws	**Carla Mendonça**
Eddie Fredericks	**Richard Moore**
Mehmet	**Gary Oliver**
Archbishop / Doctor	**Roderick Smith**

Creative Team

Director	**David Grindley**
Designer	**Jonathan Fensom**
Lighting Designer	**Jason Taylor**
Sound Designer	**Gregory Clarke**
Assistant Director	**Anna Ledwich**
Voice and Dialect Coach	**Majella Hurley**
Casting	**Gemma Hancock**
Production Manager (for RHO DELTA LTD)	**Richard Howey**
Company Stage Manager	**Patricia Davenport**
Deputy Stage Manager	**Nina Scholar**
Assistant Stage Manager	**Ruthie Philip-Smith**
Costume Supervisor	**Christina Cunningham**
Wardrobe Maintenance	**Lesley Huckstepp**
Set built by	**All Scene All Props**
'The Helping Hand' built by	**The Especial Effects Company**
Press Representative	**Becky Sayer** (020 7449 4151)

Produced by arrangement with Greg Ripley-Duggan

hampsteadtheatre would like to thank **Clone Zone** in Soho, **Chanel**, **Ellie Haddington, French Medicare, Esther-Imogen Joyce, Limbless Association, Spy Equipment, Stephen Barnett.**

In The Club was first performed at Hampstead Theatre on 25 July 2007.

Biographies

Richard Bean
Writer

Theatre includes: **Up on Roof** (Hull Truck); **Harvest** (Royal Court - Winner of the Critics' Circle Award for Best Play 2005); **Honeymoon Suite** (ETT at the Royal Court - Winner of the 2002 Pearson Award for Best New Play); **Toast** (Royal Court); **Smack Family Robinson** (Live! Theatre, Newcastle); **The God Botherers** (The Bush); **Under the Whaleback** (Royal Court - Winner of the George Devine Award 2002); **The Mentalists** (National Theatre); **Mr England** (Crucible Theatre, Sheffield).

Cast

Sian Brooke
Sasha

Theatre includes: **How To Completely Disappear And Never Be Found** (Crucible Theatre, Sheffield); **Dying City, Harvest, Just A Bloke, The One With The Oven** (Royal Court); **Midsummer Night's Dream** (RSC/ London Sinfonia); **Romeo And Juliet, King Lear, Poor Beck** (RSC); **Absolutely! Perhaps** (Wyndhams, West End). Television includes: **Cape Wrath, Hotel Babylon** (Series 2), **Housewife 49, A Touch of Frost, Foyle's War, Under the Greenwood Tree, All about George, Dinotopia.** Radio includes: **Murder on the Home Front, Dreaming of Africa.**

Dermot Canavan
Gendarme

Theatre Includes: **A Christmas Carol** (Shaw Theatre); **Merry Wives Of Windsor, Macbeth** (Oxford Shakespeare); **The Incarcerator** (Old Red Lion); **Office Suite** (Theatre Royal Bath); **Hairspray!** (Shaftsbury Theatre). Television includes: **Dalziel and Pascoe, Silent Witness, The Zoo, Where the Heart Is.**

James Fleet
Philip Wardrobe

Theatre includes: **Habeas Corpus** (Theatre Royal Bath/tour); **Mary Stuart** (Donmar Warehouse); **Three Sisters** (Playhouse Theatre); **Art** (Wyndhams); **The Late Middle Classes** (National tour); **Neville's Island** (Nottingham Playhouse); **Berenice** (National Theatre); **The Crimson Island** (The Gate); **The Churchill Play, The Taming of the Shrew, Hyde Park, The Jew of Malta, Waste, The Dillen, A New Way to Pay Old Debts, The Time of Your Life, Peter Pan, Henry IV Parts I & II, Money, The Witch of Edmonton, A Midsummer Night's Dream** (RSC). Televison includes: **Legit, Midsomer Murders, Sea of Souls, Monarch of the Glen, Promoted to Glory, Young Arthur, Fields of Gold, Brotherly Love, Chambers, Spark, Underworld, A Dance to the Music of Time, Cows, Crossing the Floor, Harry Enfield and Chums, Moll Flanders, Lord of Misrule, The Vicar of Dibley** (4 series), **Milner, Cracker, Murder Most Horrid, Running Late, The Common Pursuit, They Never Slept.** Film includes: **A Cock and Bull Story, The Phantom of the Opera, Blackball, South From Granada, Two Men Went To War, Charlotte Grey, Kevin and Perry, Milk, Frenchman's Creek, Remember Me, Eskimo Day, Butterfly Effect, The Grotesque, Sense & Sensibility, Three Steps to Heaven, Four Weddings and a Funeral, Femme Fatale, Blue Black Permanent, An Electric Moon.**

Anna Francolini
Beatrice Renard

Theatre includes: **Into The Woods** (Royal Opera House); **Caroline, Or Change, Metropolis Kabarett, Almost Like Being In Love** (National Theatre); **Six Pictures Of Lee Miller** (Minerva Theatre); **5/11** (Chichester Festival Theatre); **Spittin' Distance** (Stephen Joseph Theatre); **Acorn Antiques** (Phil MacIntyre Ents); **Romeo And Juliet** (English Touring Theatre); **The Ballad Of Little Jo** (Bridewell Theatre); **Things You Shouldn't Say Past Midnight** (Soho Theatre); **The Tempest** (A&BC Theatre Company); **Daisy Pulls It Off** (Clear Channel Entertainment); **Mahler's Conversation** (ACT Productions); **Merrily We Roll Along, Company** (Donmar Warehouse); **Floyd Collins** (Bridewell Theatre); **A Midsummer Night's Dream** (Oxford Stage Company); **Saturday Night** (Bridewell Theatre). Television includes: **Live Girls, Rome, Holby City, Lie with Me, Down To Earth, This Is Dom Joly, Jonathan Creek, Company, Mash&Peas Do Us.** Film includes: **Topsy Turvy, The Final Curtain, The Barn, Z.**

Huw Higginson
Andre

Theatre includes: **What The Butler Saw** (Hampstead Theatre/Criterion Theatre); **Abigail's Party** (Hampstead Theatre/tour/Theatre Royal Bath); **Arsenic and Old Lace** (No.1 Tour); **Lone Star** (Sydney Opera House/ Australia Tour); **Aladdin** (Malvern Festival Theatre); **Breezeblock Park, Sergeant Musgrave's Dance, Plenty** (Manchester Library); **Lone Star** (Old Red Lion); **The Voyage Of The Dawn Treader** (Vanessa Ford Tour); **Season** (Palace Westcliffe); **Bungles Of Joy** (Orange Tree); **Henry IV Part II** (RSC). Television includes: **Living It, Doctors,**

Casualty, Blessed, The Giblets, Basil Brush, Holby City, EastEnders, Casualty, Heartbeat, The Hunt, PC Garfield in **The Bill, Defrosting the Fridge, How We Used To Live, Flood Tide, Big Deal.** Film: **Jessica.**

Carol Macready
Frau Flugelhammerlein

Theatre includes: **Enjoy** (Watford Palace Theatre); **School For Scandal** (Salisbury Playhouse); **The Comedy of Errors, Cider With Rosie** (Crucible Theatre, Sheffield); **The Turn Of The Screw** (Bristol Old Vic); **The Rivals** (Compass Theatre); **The Mandate, Tales From The Vienna Woods, Edmond, The Wind In The Willows** (National Theatre); **Romeo and Juliet** (New Shakespeare Company); **Love In A Wood, Roberto Zucco, Jubilee, Bartholomew Fair, Measure For Measure** (RSC); **A Busy Day** (Bristol Old Vic/Lyric Theatre); **Pygmalion, The Playboy Of The Western World, Weekend Break** (Birmingham Rep); **School For Wives** (Almeida); **Days Of Cavafi** (Kings Head); **Habeas Corpus** (Thorndike Theatre, Leatherhead); **Orpheus Descending** (Royal Haymarket Theatre); **Absolute Hell** (Orange Tree Theatre); **Captain Oates' Left Sock, Comedy Of The Changing Years** (Royal Court). Television includes: **Doctors, Holby City, Love Lies Bleeding, Midsomer Murders, Coronation Street, Doc Martin, Trial & Retribution, Heartbeat, Dangerfield, The Bill, The Darling Buds Of May, Birds Of A Feather, EastEnders, Poirot.** Film includes: **Wondrous Oblivion, 102 Dalmatians, The Night Is Young, Quills, The Pirates of Penzance, The Scarlet Pimpernel, Hellraisers, The Village.** Radio includes: **Felix Holt, The Radical, My Cousin Rachel, The Lady Bower Reservoir, Dixon Of Dock Green, With Great Pleasure At Christmas.**

Carla Mendonça
Nicola Daws

Theatre includes: **Ugly Rumours** (Tricycle Theatre); **Comic Cuts** (Salisbury Playhouse/Lyric Theatre Hammersmith); **Sod** (Pleasance, Edinburgh Festival); **As You Like It, King Lear, Measure For Measure, Don Juan** (Oxford Stage Company/tour/Riverside Studios); **Time and The Conways** (Derby Playhouse); **Twelfth Night, Educating Rita** (Oldham Coliseum); **Daisy Pulls It Off** (Globe/GielgudTheatre); Television includes: **Roman's Empire, My Parents Are Aliens** (6 seasons), **My Dad's The Prime Minister, Spark, Harry Enfield and Chums, French and Saunders, Saturday Live, Bottom, The Lenny Henry Show, The Young Ones.** Film: **The Red Peppers.** Radio includes: **Three Off The Tee, Double Income No Kids Yet, People Like Us, Audio Diaries, Paris London.**

Richard Moore
Eddie Fredericks

Theatre includes: **Winters Tale, Pericles, Waiting For Godot, Under Milk Wood, Lynchville, Dumb Waiter, Merry Wives Of Windsor, Two Gentlemen Of Verona, Romeo And Juliet, Henry V, Richard II, Troilus And Cressida, Midsummer Night's Dream, Hamlet, As You Like It** (RSC); **Dead Funny, Ink and Urine, Merry Wives of Windsor, The Visit, The Silver King, Three Men In A Boat** (Chichester Festival Theatre); **Rosencrantz & Guildenstern Are Dead, An Evening With Charles Dickens** (Theatr Clwyd/tour); **King Lear** (Theatr Clwyd); **Two Clouds Over Eden** (Royal Exchange, Manchester); **Twelfth Night, Hay Fever, Educating Rita, Passion Play, Hedda Gabler, School For Scandal, The Cherry Orchard, Much Ado About Nothing, Hamlet, Taming Of The Shrew** (Leicester Haymarket); **Merry Wives of**

Windsor (National Theatre); **Macbeth, The Connection, The Samaritan, Hans Kolhaas, The Tribades, Quantrille In Lawrence, The Passion Of Dracula** (London/West End); **The Birdwatchers, King Lear, As You Like It** (Australia). Television includes: **Gold Plated, Emmerdale, Born & Bred, Where The Heart Is, Heartbeat, The Mayor Of Casterbridge, Nearest And Dearest, Band Of Gold, Wycliffe, House Of Elliot, Enemy At The Door, Good As Gold, Chancer, The Professionals, The Likely Lads, Z Cars.** Film includes: **Fanny and Elvis, The Human Bomb, Blue Juice, Deadly Advice, Robin Hood, Death Of A Son, Lady Jane, Juggernaut, The Offence, The Raging Moon.**

Gary Oliver
Mehmet

Theatre includes: **The Royal Hunt Of The Sun, Tales from Vienna Woods, A Streetcar Named Desire, Sing Yer Heart Out For The Lads, The Cherry Orchard** (National Theatre); **Julius Caesar** (RSC/Lyric Hammersmith); **Festen** (Almeida Theatre); **The Two Gentleman of Verona** (RSC); **Black Milk, Terrorism** (Royal Court); **Angels In America** (Manchester Library Theatre), **Squash** (Old Red Lion); **A Comedy Of Errors** (RSC /Young Vic Theatre); **Salvation: Raft Of The Medusa** (The Gate); **Unidentified Human Remains & The True Nature Of Love** (Manchester Royal Exchange); **The Fire Raisers, The Slow Approach of Night** (Arts Threshold); **The Lizzie Play** (Theatre Clwyd/tour); **Look Back In Anger, King Lear, Endgame** (Wink Productions); **Romeo & Juliet** (Factotum Touring Co); **Shoemakers** (BAC/Ragazzi Theatre Co); **Puppet Play Of Don Christabel** (Ragazzi Theatre Co); **The Importance Of Being Earnest** (Stephen Joseph Theatre).

Roderick Smith
Archbishop / Doctor

Theatre includes: **The Indian Boy** (RSC); **Journey's End** (New Ambassadors); **Gone To Earth** (Shared Experience); **The God Botherers** (The Bush); **Pat and Margaret** (Salisbury Playhouse); **The Glee Club** (The Bush/The Duchess); **Tragedy: A Tragedy** (The Gate); **Best Mates** (National Theatre/tour); **The Winter's Tale** (Southwark Playhouse); **Enjoy** (Nottingham Playhouse); **The Birthday Party, Tales From Hollywood, Antigone, Neaptide, Garden Of England, True Dare Kiss, Command Or Promise** (National Theatre); **The Wicked Cooks, Outskirts** (Birmingham Rep); **The Beaux' Stratagem, Rhinoceros** (The Nuffield Southampton); **Artists And Admirers, The Changeling, One Fine Day** (Riverside Studios) ; **The Fool** (Royal Court). Television includes: **The Bill, Family Affairs, Judge John Deed, The Rotters' Club, Inspector Lynley Mysteries, The Story Of Tracy Beaker, The Basil Brush Show, Holby City, Doctors,** Sgt. Keith Lardner in **Dangerfield** (six series). Film includes: **Sylvia, In Search Of Gregory.**

Creative Team

David Grindley
Director

Theatre includes: **What The Butler Saw** (Hampstead Theatre/West End); **Abigail's Party** (Hampstead Theatre/ West End – Best Revival nominee, 2003 Olivier Awards); **Journey's End** (Belasco, Broadway NYC - Best Revival 2007 Tony, Outer Critics Circle and Drama Desk Awards; New York Drama Critics Circle Special Citation); **Honour** (Wyndhams, West End); **The Philanthropist** (Donmar Warehouse); **Some Girl(s)** (Gielgud Theatre, West End); **National Anthems** (Old Vic Theatre); **Journey's End** (Comedy Theatre/ Duke Of York's/New Ambassadors/tour – Best Revival nominee, 2005 Olivier Awards); **Excuses!** (Actors Touring Theatre/ Soho Theatre/tour); **Single Spies** (Theatre Royal Bath Productions/tour); **Mental** (Edinburgh Suite Assembly Rooms); **Having A Ball** (Richard Temple Productions/tour); **Wait Until Dark, Things We Do For Love** (Royal Theatre Northampton); **The Erpingham Camp** (Liverpool Everyman/Edinburgh Festival); **Alarms & Excursions** (Argentina); **Richard III** (Mercury Theatre Colchester); **The Real Inspector Hound & Black Comedy** (National Tour); **Loot** (West End/Tour). Future Projects include: **Pygmalion** (Roundabout Theatre Company, NYC).

Jonathan Fensom
Designer

Theatre includes: **What the Butler Saw** (Hampstead Theatre/West End); **Born Bad, In Arabia We'd All Be Kings, Abigail's Party** (Hampstead Theatre); **Love's Labours Lost** (Globe); **Journey's End** (West End/ Broadway); **Big White Fog** (Almeida); **Kindertransport, Breakfast with**

Emma (Shared Experience); **The Tempest** (The Tron Theatre); **Charley's Aunt** (Oxford Playhouse); **The Faith Healer** (The Gate, Dublin/Broadway); **Smaller** (West End/tour); **Burn / Citizenship / Chatroom** (National Theatre); **God of Hell** (Donmar Warehouse); **Some Girl(s)** (West End); **The Sugar Syndrome, Duck, Talking to Terrorists** (Royal Court/tour); **National Anthems** (Old Vic); **The Lady in the Van** (Theatre Royal Bath/tour); **Twelfth Night** (West End); **Cloud Nine** (Crucible Theatre, Sheffield); **Candide** (Oxford Playhouse); **M.A.D., Little Baby Nothing** (Bush Theatre); **Small Family Business, Little Shop of Horrors** (West Yorkshire Playhouse); **My Night With Reg and Dealer's Choice** (Birmingham Rep); **Be My Baby** (Soho Theatre/tour); **After the Dance, Hay Fever** (Oxford Stage Company); **The Mentalists** (National Theatre); **So Long Life** (Theatre Royal Bath/tour) **Wozzeck** (Birmingham Opera/European tour); **Spike** (Nuffield, Southampton). Other work includes: **The Rivals** (Northcott, Exeter); **Passing Places** (Derby Playhouse/Greenwich Theatre); **Erpingham Camp** (Edinburgh Assembly Rooms/tour); **Alarms and Excursions** (Producciones Alejandro Romay, Argentina); **A Streetcar Named Desire, Richard III, Bouncers** (Mercury Theatre, Colchester); **East** (Vaudeville, West End/tour); **Backroom** (Bush Theatre); **Dangerous Corner, The Government Inspector** (Watermill Theatre); **Immaculate Misconception** (New End Theatre); **Take Away** (Lyric Hammersmith/tour); **Richard III** (Pleasance tour to Oldenburg, Chemnitz, Germany); **Ghetto** (Riverside Studios); **Roots and Wings** (Sherman Theatre), **Yusupov** (Andrew Lloyd Webber's Sydmonton Festival); **The Importance of Being Earnest, Billy Liar, Wait Until Dark** (Salisbury Playhouse); **September Tide** (King's Head/tour/Comedy Theatre, West End); **Cinderella and Stevie** (Dukes Theatre, Lancaster). Television and film includes: **tvSSFBM EHKL, Arena, Tomorrow La Scala.** Jonathan was Associate Designer on Disney's **The Lion King**, which premiered at the New Amsterdam Theatre on Broadway and has subsequently opened worldwide.

Jason Taylor
Lighting Designer

Theatre includes: **Journey's End** (West End/National tour/Broadway – winner of the 2007 Tony Award for Best Revival); **High Society, The Letter, The New Statesman** (UK tours); **Burn / Citizenship / Chatroom** (National Theatre); **What Every Woman Knows** (Manchester Royal Exchange); **The God of Hell** (Donmar Warehouse). Forthcoming projects include: **Victory, How the Other Half Loves** (Theatre Royal Bath); **Pygmalion** (Roundabout Theatre Company, NY); **Ideal Husband** (Manchester Royal Exchange). Jason also designed the lighting for Regent's Park Open Air Theatre summer season in 2006 and 2007.

Gregory Clarke
Sound Designer

Theatre includes: **The Glass Room, Everything Is Illuminated, Clever Dick, The Schuman Plan, What the Butler Saw, When the Night Begins, The Maths Tutor, Abigail's Party, The Dead Eye Boy, Buried Alive, Tender** (Hampstead Theatre); **Equus** (Gielgud); **Journey's End** (London/tour/Broadway, New York Drama Desk Award winner for outstanding sound design); **A Voyage Round My Father, Honour** (Wyndhams); **The Philanthropist** (Donmar Warehouse); **Hayfever, Lady Windermere's Fan, The Royal Family** (Theatre Royal, Haymarket); **The Home Place, Whose Life is it**

Anyway? (Comedy Theatre); **The Emperor Jones** and **The Chairs** (Gate); **And Then There Were None, Some Girls** (Gielgud); **Waiting For Godot** (New Ambassadors); **What the Butler Saw** (Criterion); **The Dresser** (Duke Of York's); **Amy's View, You Never Can Tell** (Garrick); **National Anthems** (Old Vic); **Betrayal** (Duchess); **Abigail's Party** (New Ambassadors); **Mum's the Word** (Albery); **Song Of Singapore** (Mayfair); **No Man's Land, Tristan and Yseult, The Emperor Jones** (National Theatre); **Great Expectations, Coriolanus, The Merry Wives of Windsor, Tantalus, Cymbeline** (RSC); **Measure For Measure, Pygmalion, Little Nell, Victory, Habeas Corpus, Miss Julie, Private Lives, Much Ado About Nothing, You Never Can Tell, Design for Living, Betrayal, Fight for Barbara, As You Like It** (The Peter Hall Company); **The Changeling** (Barbican); **Nights at the Circus** (Lyric Theatre Hammersmith/tour); **Insignificance** (Lyceum Theatre, Sheffield); **My Boy Jack** (National tour); **Lady Be Good, Macbeth, The Boyfriend, Twelfth Night, Cymbeline, HMS Pinafore, Henry IV Part I, A Midsummer Night's Dream, The Two Gentlemen of Verona, Loves Labour's Lost** (Open Air Theatre, Regent's Park); **Seven Doors, Semi-Detached, Pal Joey, Heartbreak House, A Small Family Business, I Caught My Death in Venice, Nathan the Wise, Song of Singapore, Nymph Errant** (Chichester); **As You Like It** (US tour); **Office Suite, Present Laughter, Old Times, How The Other Half Loves** (Theatre Royal Bath).

Anna Ledwich
Assistant Director

Theatre includes: **Awakenings** (La Mama, Melbourne); **Yellowing** (Harrow Arts Centre/Theatre 503); **Poet No.7** (Theatre 503/Dublin International Fringe Festival); **Roulette** (Finborough Theatre); **GBS** (Theatre 503); European premiere of three short plays by Tennessee Williams under the title of **Lovely and Misfit** (Trafalgar Studios). Anna was Associate Director to Yvonne McDevitt on **Brussels Manifesto** (Espace Scarabeus, Brussels) and Associate Director of Theatre 503 from 2005–2006.

hampsteadtheatre is one of the UK's leading new writing venues housed in a magnificent purpose-built state-of-the-art theatre – a company that is fast approaching its fiftieth year of operation.

hampsteadtheatre has a mission: to find, develop, and produce new plays to the highest possible standards, for as many people as we can encourage to see them. Its work is both national and international in its scope and ambition.

hampsteadtheatre exists to take risks and to discover the talent of the future. New writing is our passion. We consistently create the best conditions for writers to flourish and are rewarded with diverse, award-winning and far-reaching plays.

The list of playwrights who had their early work produced at **hampstead**theatre who are now filling theatres all over the country and beyond include Mike Leigh, Michael Frayn, Brian Friel, Terry Johnson, Hanif Kureishi, Simon Block, Abi Morgan, Rona Munro, Tamsin Oglesby, Harold Pinter, Philip Ridley, Shelagh Stephenson, debbie tucker green, Crispin Whittell and Roy Williams. The careers of actors Jude Law, Alison Steadman, Jane Horrocks and Rufus Sewell were launched at **hampstead**theatre.

Each year the theatre invites the most exciting writers around to write for us. At least half of these playwrights will be emerging writers who are just hitting their stride – writers who we believe are on the brink of establishing themselves as important new voices. We also ask mid-career and mature playwrights to write for us on topics they are burning to explore.

The success of **hampstead**theatre is yours to support

Since opening our stunning award-winning building, we have presented sixteen world premieres and twenty-one London premieres. We have commissioned thirty-two writers, transferred two plays to the West End, and six of our playwrights have won prestigious Most Promising Playwright awards. We also have one of the most extensive education and participation programmes of all theatres in London.

Our artistic achievements have inspired increasing critical and commercial success. This has been made possible by the many individuals, trusts and companies that have already chosen to invest in our creativity. To secure our bright future we need your support.

If you would like more information about supporting **hampstead**theatre and helping us to nurture the new talents and audiences of the future, please email development@hampsteadtheatre.com or call Tamzin Robertson on 020 7449 4171.

hampsteadtheatre would like to thank the following for their support:

Abbey Charitable Trust; Acacia Charitable Trust; Anglo American; Arimathea Charitable Trust; Arts & Business; Awards for All; The Alchemy Foundation; Auerbach Trust Charity; BBC Children in Need; Bennetts Associates; Big Lottery Fund; Blick Rothenberg; Bridge House Estates Trust Fund; Community Chest; Community Fund; The John S Cohen Foundation; Coutts Charitable Trust; D'Oyly Carte Charitable Trust; The Dorset Foundation; The Eranda Foundation; The Ernest Cook Trust; European Association of Jewish Culture; Garrick Charitable Trust; Gerald Ronson Foundation; GHP Group; Goldschmidt and Howland; The Goldsmiths Company; The Hampstead & Highgate Express; Help a London Child; Harold Hyam Wingate Foundation; The Jack Petchey Foundation; Jacobs Charitable Trust; John Lyon's Charitable Trust; Lloyds TSB Foundation for England and Wales; Kennedy Leigh Charitable Trust; Local Network Fund; Mackintosh Foundation; Markson Pianos; Milly Apthorp Charitable Trust; The Mirianog Trust; The Morel Trust: The No¨el Coward Foundation; Notes Productions Ltd; Ocado; The Ormonde & Mildred Duveen Trust; Parkheath Estates: The Paul Hamlyn Foundation: The Rayne Foundation; Reed Elsevier; Richard Grand Foundation; Richard Reeves Foundation; Royal Victoria Hall Foundation; Samuel French; The Shoresh Foundation; Sir John Cass' Foundation; Society for Theatre Research; Solomon Taylor Shaw: Sweet and Maxwell; Karl Sydow; Towry Law; The Vintners' Company; World Jewish Relief; Charles Wolfson Foundation.

hampsteadtheatre would also like to thank the numerous individuals who have supported the theatre through our Luminary scheme:

capital campaign supporters

hampsteadtheatre would like to thank the following donors who kindly contributed to the Capital Campaign, enabling us to build our fantastic new home:

Mr Robert Adams
Mr Robert Ainscow
Mrs Farah Alaghband
Mr W Aldwinckle
Mr Mark Allison
Anonymous
Mrs Klari Atkin
Mr William Atkins
Mr and Mrs Daniel and Pauline Auerbach
Mr David Aukin
Sir Alan Ayckbourn
Mr George Bailey
Mr Christopher Beard
Mr Eric Beecham
Mrs Lucy Ben-Levi
Mr Alan Bennett
Mr and Mrs Rab Bennetts
Mr Roger Berlind
Ms Vicky Biles
Mr Michael Blakemore
Mr Simon Block
Mr A Bloomfield
Mr John Bolton
Mr Peter Borender
Mr and Mrs Rob and Colleen Brand
Mr Matthew Broadbent
Mr Alan Brodie
Dr John and Dorothy Brook
Mr Leonard Bull
Mr and Mrs Paul and Ossie Burger
Ms Kathy Burke
Mr O Burstin
Ms Deborah Buzan
Mr Charles Caplin
Sir Trevor and Susan Chinn
Mr Martin Cliff
Mr Michael Codron
Mr and Mrs Denis Cohen
Dr David Cohen
Mr David Cornwell
Mr and Mrs Sidney and Elizabeth Corob
Mr and Mrs John Crosfield
Miss Nicci Crowther
Ms Hilary Dane
Mr and Mrs Ralph Davidson
Mr and Mrs Gerald Davidson
Mrs Deborah Davis
Mr Edwin Davison
Mr David Day
Ms Frankie de Freitas
Mr and Mrs David and Jose Dent
Professor Christopher and Elizabeth Dickinson
Sir Harry Djanogly

Ms Lindsay Duncan
Mr David Dutton
Mrs Myrtle Ellenbogen
Mr Michael Elwyn
Mr Tom Erhardt
Sir Richard Eyre
Mr Peter Falk
Ms Nina Finburgh
Mr and Mrs George and Rosamund Fokschaner
Ms Lisa Forrell
Mr N Forsyth
Mr Freddie Fox
Mr Michael Frayn
Mr Norman Freed
Mr Conrad Freedman
Mr and Mrs Robert and Elizabeth Freeman
Mr and Mrs Jeremy and Susan Freeman
Mr and Mrs Brian Friel
Mr Arnold Fulton
Mr and Mrs Michael and Jacqueline Gee
Mr and Mrs Jonathan and Jacqueline Gestetner
Mr Desmond Goch
Mr Anthony Goldstein
Mr Andrew Goodman
Ms Niki Gorick
Mrs Katerina Gould
Lord and Lady Grabiner
Mr and Mrs Jonathan Green
Mr and Mrs David Green
Mrs Susan Green
Mr Nicholas Greenstone
Mr Michael Gross
Mr and Mrs Paul Hackworth
Dr Peter and Elaine Hallgarten
Miss Susan Hampshire
Mr Christopher Hampton
Mr Laurence Harbottle
Sir David Hare
Lady Pamela Harlech
Mr Paul Harris
Mr John Harrison
Mr Howard Harrison
Mr Jonathan Harvey
Sir Maurice Hatter
Mr Marc Hauer
Dr Samuel Hauer
Mr and Mrs Michael and Morven Heller
Mr Philip Hobbs
Mr and Mrs Robin and Inge Hyman
Mr Nicolas Hytner

Ms Phoebe Isaacs
Mr Michael Israel
Professor Howard and Sandra Jacobs
Mr and Mrs Max Jacobs
Dr C Kaplanis
Mrs Patricia Karet
Baroness Helena Kennedy
Mrs Ann Kieran
Mr Jeremy King
Mr Peter Knight
Sir Eddie Kulukundis
Ms Belinda Lang
Mr and Mrs Edward Lee
Mrs Janette Lesser
Lady Diane Lever
Mr Daniel Levy
Mr Peter Levy
Sir Sydney and Lady Lipworth
Mrs Alyssa Lovegrove
Ms Sue MacGregor
Mr S Magee
Mr Fouad Malouf
Mr and Mrs Lee Manning
Mr and Mrs Thomas and Karen Mautner
Mr and Mrs David and Sandra Max
Mrs June McCall
Mr John McFadden
Mr Ewan McGregor
Mr and Mrs David Meller
Mr Raymond Mellor
Mr Anthony Minghella
Mr and Mrs David Mirvish
Mr and Mrs Mark Mishon
Mr and Mrs Edward and Diana Mocatta
Mr and Mrs Gary Monnickendam
Mrs and Mrs David and Sandra Montague
Mr Peter Morris
Mr and Mrs Ian Morrison
Mr Andrew Morton
Lady Sara Morton
Mr Gabriel Moss QC
Mr and Mrs Terence Mugliston
Mr and Mrs Roger and Bridget Myddelton
Mr Stewart Nash
Mr James Nederlander
Mr John Newbigin
Sir Trevor Nunn
Mr T Owen
Mr and Mrs Simon and Midge Palley
Mr Barrie Pearson

hampsteadtheatre would also like to thank the many generous donors
who we are unable to list individually.

creative learning at **hampstead**theatre

Our creative learning programme is a thriving part of **hampstead**theatre's work. We aim to celebrate all aspects of the creative process through a vibrant and diverse range of workshops based around our busy programme of theatre. This experience is offered to all people of all ages from all sectors of the community.

In the last year (April 06 to March 07) our programme's outcomes included:
- 11,000 participants, of which 58% from a BME background, at 595 events.
- 75 educational projects delivered at **hampstead**theatre and out in school and community settings.
- 83 educational performances in the Michael Frayn Space.

the **heat&light** company
(**hampstead**theatre's youth theatre)

Budding writers, performers, directors, stage managers and technicians come together to explore the power and potential of theatre. Each term a new **heat&light** company is formed, consisting of four groups of young people: year groups 7-9, 10-11, 12-13 and 18-25 year olds.

The **heat&light** company is free to all participants and produces twelve performances a year. The artistic direction of each youth theatre project is led by the Creative Direction Team, which consists of members of the **heat&light** company. Each member is given a specific responsibility mirroring the roles in **hampstead**theatre's artistic, production and administration teams.

schools

We work in schools throughout the day with breakfast drama clubs, lunchtime writing clubs and after school scriptwriting clubs. All of our activities in the schools programme are designed to stimulate creativity, improve literacy and encourage as many children and young people as possible to engage with new writing in theatre and understand its relevance to their lives.

Each year lunchtime and after school writing clubs produce over 300 script-in-hand performances of plays and stories, some of which go on to form the basis of **heat&light** productions. In-school scriptwriting classes are currently funded by a number of charitable trusts, giving young people across north London the opportunity to develop their skills, self-esteem and confidence.

follow spot

Our schools audience programme provides teacher resources, talks and training which reveal the creative practice behind productions at **hampstead**theatre. The programme aims to stimulate creativity and offer alternative strategies for learning, to explore the techniques used and the issues raised, and to increase understanding of the creative industries and career possibilities.

Visit our website www.hampsteadtheatre.com for more information and the Follow Spot schedule.

reaching out

We also deliver special projects in a variety of community settings, including hospitals, community centres and other places where theatre and playwriting may not be a natural part of life.

We work with ESOL students from Westminster Kingsway College, using drama games and improvisation to support literacy. Our community drama group, Generator, engages adults from a wide range of backgrounds in devising and performance projects.

get in touch

For more information about any of our projects, or about how to join any of our participation programmes, visit our website, talk to us on 020 7449 4200 dept 4 or email creativelearning@hampsteadtheatre.com.

make a difference

We are keen to create innovative and mutually beneficial connections between ourselves and others. If you would like to become more closely involved and support specific projects, please email or call Tamzin Robertson at development@hampsteadtheatre.com or 020 7449 4171.

hampsteadtheatre staff and company

Richard Bean

IN THE CLUB

A Political Sex Farce for the Stage

OBERON BOOKS
LONDON

First published in 2007 by Oberon Books Ltd
521 Caledonian Road, London N7 9RH
Tel: 020 7607 3637 / Fax: 020 7607 3629
email: info@oberonbooks.com
www.oberonbooks.com

A catalogue record for this book is available from the British
Library.

ISBN: 1 84002 757 6 / 978-1-84002-757-0

'I love France and Belgium, but we must not allow ourselves to be pulled down to that level.'

Winston Churchill, 1953

Characters

PHILIP WARDROBE MEP

ALEXANDRIA TOGUSHEV (SASHA)

FRAU FLUGELHAMMERLEIN

MEHMET AZIZ

BEATRICE RENARD

EDDIE FREDERICKS

ANDRE PICQ

NICOLA DAWS

Also:
Gendarme, Doctor, Archbishop, Priests

The function suite of a superior Strasbourg hotel. In the back wall there are double doors which are the main entrance doors to the suite. When these double doors are open the doors to a lift can be seen. Downstage left is a door which leads to a double room with a picture window view of the Strasbourg Parliament building as a feature. This is Bed 1. This room also has an en-suite bathroom: Bath 1. Downstage right is a door which opens into a smaller bedroom with en-suite bathroom (Bed 2 and Bath 2). Upstage right is a door to a walk-in linen cupboard. Against the wall stage left are two side tables. On one of these is a laptop computer and various papers, a fax and phone etc. On one wall is a pull-down (ie rolled up) film screen. A sofa, armchair and coffee table are set downstage centre.

Act One

The present. Early morning. As the audience take their seats the occasional beep comes from the computer as emails arrive. The door to Bed 1 is open and faint sounds of a jacuzzi can be heard. A mobile phone goes off in the central area. Enter PHILIP WARDROBE (MEP) from Bed 1, in dressing gown, looking hung-over. He has a can of athlete's foot powder in one hand. He searches for the mobile.

PHILIP: (*On the phone.*) Nicola! Darling! For the last time, I am not having an affair!

Enter SASHA from Bed 1 wearing a short dressing gown and a towel round her hair. She starts to head for Bed 2 but is distracted by newly arrived emails and the coffee.

I am totally and incredibly not interested in other women!

He sneaks a lech at the half-naked SASHA as she reads faxes.

NO! Every other male member, so to speak, of the European Parliament does have a 'Strasbourg wife' and some of them have a 'Brussels wife' on top, or underneath, but I do not, I have you, a 'Kettering wife'…Nicola!

The call is over. PHILIP pours himself a coffee and sits and begins to powder his toes.

(*Holding his head.*) How the hell did I find this place last night?

SASHA: Les Aviateurs closes at three in the morning so I sent a car with instructions to collect a man sitting on the kerb singing 'You'll Never Walk Alone'.

PHILIP: Sasha, you're a credit to the whole concept of illegal immigration. What were you doing in my bathroom?

SASHA: There's a problem with the plumbing in my room.

PHILIP: Never! It's costing me an arm and a leg this place!

SASHA: It's not costing you anything.

PHILIP: Figure of speech.

PHILIP stands and begins to inspect the suite, opening doors etc.

If someone five years ago had said to me – 'Do you want to be an MEP *or* do you want to win the lottery?' – stupidly I would have gone for the lottery win. I LOVE being an MEP. It's a win win situation. The people of Northamptonshire don't know who I am, and I don't know who they are.

He starts having a look around.

Classy place this.

SASHA: It's the most expensive hotel in Strasbourg.

PHILIP: The Turks are happy to pay.

He opens the main double doors to reveal a group of priests/vicars standing by the lift.

Bonjour!

PHILIP closes the doors. He thinks for a moment then goes to the door of Bed 2.

(*At the door of Bed 2.*) Can I have a look?

(*Off.*) Godda be one of the finest decisions of my political career, getting on the Turkey committee.

SASHA: There's an email from Mehmet Aziz.

PHILIP: (*Re-appearing. Clapping his hands.*) No politics today. Nicola's flying in for…you know.

SASHA: Today?

PHILIP: Oh yes. Monday the twelfth of March two thousand and seven will go down in history as OVARIES MONDAY – the day that Philip Wardrobe MEP personally intervened to reverse the disaster of Europe's falling birth rate.

SASHA: Mehmet says 'Prime Minister Erdogan is extremely angry what did you say to him?'

PHILIP: I only asked him which one of Turkey's barking mad mullahs came up with the idea of three years in prison for slagging off Turkey. Reasonable question. When you're a bit pissed.

SASHA: You're talking about Turkey's article 301. That was Erdogan's own idea.

PHILIP: Fuck! I'm busting my balls going around telling Europe that Turkey is an incredibly cuddly liberal democracy and what do the Turks do, they start banging up any Turk daft enough to say, 'Actually I think Turkey's a bit shit!'

SASHA: Mehmet wants a meeting this morning.

PHILIP: No!

SASHA: You can't say no, Turkey are paying for this suite.

PHILIP: OK! Say yes then. And in my diary write – Mehmet, nine o'clock and then draw a box around the afternoon and call it 'face to face meeting – egg and sperm'. Me and Nicola.

SASHA: Do you think Turkey'll stop your money?

PHILIP: I'd miss it. Kaw! Beach villa; ski lodge; penthouse flat in Ankara that gets hoovered twice a week by the current Miss Turkey.

SASHA: If Turkey joins the EU, one in four Europeans will be Muslim.

PHILIP: One in four?! Bloody hell! That's nearly a quarter!

SASHA: I don't know why you socialists don't exploit the split in the EPP on the Turkey issue.

PHILIP: Eh?

SASHA: The EPP slash ED grouping is the biggest party in the Parliament with two hundred whatever seats –

PHILIP: – two hundred and seventy-seven.

SASHA: And your Socialist party is second

PHILIP: – two hundred and eighteen.

SASHA: But the split in the democrats is already there in the name. EPP slash ED. The EPP are basically Christian Democrats panicking about Turkey because they see it as a Trojan Horse for radical Islam, but the European Democrats, the ED, of the EPP slash ED, are only interested in free market economics and look to Turkey to provide endless cheap labour. If you –

PHILIP: – me?

SASHA: The socialists – if you pressure the EPP slash ED on Turkey that split will open up and you could destroy them, and then deliver a truly socialist Europe.

PHILIP: If you're you going to be like this all day I'm going back to bed.

Knock at the door. PHILIP opens the door. ANDRE stands there in a boiler suit. He has a moustache and the trappings of a plumber.

ANDRE: Bonjour mademoiselle.

SASHA: Bonjour.

ANDRE: Il y a un petit problème de plomberie?

SASHA: Dans la deuxième chambre. Deux minutes s'il vous plaît.

SASHA goes off to change in Bed 2.

PHILIP: Elle a besoin d'habiller.

ANDRE: D'accord! English?

26

PHILIP: Yup. Sit down. Philip Wardrobe.

They shake.

ANDRE: Andre Picq. I'm Belgian.

PHILIP: Oh. Bad luck.

ANDRE and PHILIP sit on the sofa. PHILIP administers powder to his foot.

ANDRE: Athlete's foot?

PHILIP: Yes.

ANDRE: Me too. You have it on both feet?

PHILIP: Yup.

ANDRE: Me too. Athlete's feet.

PHILIP: In English we don't say 'athlete's feet'. Technically what I've got here is athlete's foot twice.

ANDRE takes a twiglet from the bowl, snaps it in half and gives it to PHILIP.

ANDRE: Put one of these between each toe. You need to get air to the skin.

PHILIP: Twenty seconds ago I thought you were a mad person but that's actually an incredibly not bad idea.

PHILIP sticks a half twiglet between two toes. SASHA comes out of Bed 2.

SASHA: D'accord.

SASHA stares at PHILIP's twigletted feet.

PHILIP: I'm aerating my toes. This bowl of twiglets is now for medicinal use only.

ANDRE goes into Bed 2 but finds any excuses for hanging around in the main room. He runs poly-pipe from Bath 1 to Bath 2 and uses an extravagant amount of duct tape to stick it to the floor.

SASHA: I've had a brilliant idea.

PHILIP takes her to one side as if to coach her in something basic.

PHILIP: No. You're my stagiaire. When you have a brilliant idea, it is actually my idea. So tell me, what is this incredibly brilliant idea of yours that I've just had?

SASHA: A letter bomb.

PHILIP: Shh! Why would I want to send a letter bomb to the Turkish Prime Minister?

During the next SASHA takes a jiffy bag from her desk.

SASHA: You send the letter bomb to yourself. There've been three bombs discovered in the post room in the last month.

PHILIP: Who in the post room is so important that they're getting letter bombs?

SASHA: Boris Yeltsin was going for re-election and he arranged for his bodyguard to spray his limousine with bullets, so it looked like he'd survived an attempt on his life.

PHILIP: Oh! It's a Russian idea is it!? If Russian ideas were that good we'd all be living on pickled beetroot, drinking petrol and shagging our sisters.

ANDRE: He won the election!

SASHA: Only people who are effecting change make enemies. It shows the Turks that you have been effective, on their behalf.

PHILIP: This is undeniably one of the best ideas of yours I've had for yonks.

SASHA hands a jiffy bag to PHILIP who holds it and looks at it.

SASHA: I'll address it to you and have it left at reception. The Turkish ambassador can bring it up himself.

SASHA picks up diary.

What time's Nicola flying over?

PHILIP: She's having a new hair system installed at eleven o'clock in London, Heathrow by two, should be here by four.

SASHA: Is she staying the night?

PHILIP: No. She's speaking at some human rights conference first thing tomorrow so she's going to get the nine o'clock back to London tonight.

SASHA: So the egg slash sperm meeting has to be this afternoon. Would it help if I took the afternoon off?

PHILIP: Good idea.

ANDRE: Your wife is a very busy woman?

PHILIP: Partner. Never married.

ANDRE: Me too. Can I suggest flowers?

PHILIP: Yes. Order some roses eh Sash!

SASHA: (*Getting online.*) OK. Message?

PHILIP: The usual.

SASHA: 'If I catch my furry fox –

PHILIP: – in my chicken coup –

SASHA: – watch out, there'll be more than broken eggs. Love, the cockerel.'

PHILIP: Cock.

SASHA: Cock?

PHILIP: Yeah.

ANDRE: You are trying for a baby?

PHILIP: Yeah.

ANDRE: Me too. We have been trying one year now. Gonda and I.

PHILIP: Two years.

ANDRE: How old is your partner?

PHILIP: Forty-two.

ANDRE: Gonda is thirty-seven. She rings me, half-eleven o'clock in the morning, I am at work, I am ready! Come home now! She says –

The beep of an arriving email.

SASHA: (*Reading an email from the screen.*) Madame Beatrice Renard. She calls you 'Cherie –'

PHILIP: Oh no!

SASHA: Was she in Les Aviateurs last night?

PHILIP: Yeah. But it started last week when I did that talk to her Women's Committee. They loved me. After – I had lunch with Beatrice, a bottle of wine, and she tells me that she's just been dumped by Mehmet.

SASHA: Mehmet?! The Turkish Ambassador?

PHILIP: Apparently, they got bladdered together one night and ended up in the sack.

SASHA: Mehmet can't drink. He's a Muslim. And he's a married man!?

PHILIP: His copy of the Qur'an has got several pages missing. Cut a long story short, at this lunch she's incredibly on the rebound from Mehmet so she starts getting frisky with me right there in the restaurant.

SASHA: And you slept with her?

PHILIP: It was raining, and I didn't have anything else to do. But I resisted.

SASHA: You resisted?!

PHILIP: Hard to believe isn't it. But I did. And she's been chasing me ever since.

SASHA: (*Reading email.*) 'I would love coffee with you this morning.'

PHILIP: Get rid of her! Tell her I died.

Another email beeps its arrival.

SASHA: What is this?

(*Translating on the hoof.*) Under no circumstances turn off my father's machine de soutien de la vie…life support machine. If you do so without my permission I'll sue you until your eyes bleed. Beatrice Renard.

PHILIP: Oh very nice.

SASHA: She's sent it to us by mistake. Is she nuts?

PHILIP: Does Dolly Parton sleep on her back?

PHILIP takes an interest in this email. Whether hard copy or on screen.

I didn't know her father was dying. He owns Monsieur Bricolage. That's three hundred DIY superstores throughout France. That's a lot of nails.

The phone rings. SASHA answers.

SASHA: (*On phone.*) Yes…she's on her way up is she? Thank you.

PHILIP: Who the hell's coming up? Not Beatrice?

SASHA: Who would you least want to see you like this?

PHILIP: The Socialist whip? Frau Flugelhammerlein. Aaaagghhh!

PHILIP picks out the twiglets from between his toes and puts them back in the bowl, then rushes into Bed 1. SASHA does a bit of tidying up, hiding empty wine bottles etc.

I hardly slept last night.

SASHA: Hitler ran the Third Reich on five hours a night.

PHILIP: (*Off.*) Margaret Thatcher only needed four – not to run the Third Reich – though it felt like it at the time.

Knock at the door. SASHA waits until PHILIP is safely out of the way in Bed 1. Enter FRAU FLUGELHEMMERLEIN. She oozes power.

FRAU: Morgen Sasha. Where is he? I don't have long.

SASHA: Yes Frau Flugelhammerlein.

She stands down stage near the coffee table, eyeing the twiglets. ANDRE moves the twiglets and puts them on a side table stage left. SASHA knocks on Bed 1 door.

Mr Wardrobe! Frau –

Enter PHILIP, immaculately dressed and looking brilliant.

PHILIP: – Guten Morgen, Freda. Wie geht's?!

FRAU hands PHILIP a document. FRAU notices ANDRE.

FRAU: The attendance records for the Party of European Socialists for the last year.

PHILIP: Ha! Did I win? Not good eh?

FRAU: If you were a horse I'd shoot you myself.

PHILIP: You couldn't do that, you'd be in breach of the council directive 93/119 on the protection of animals at time of slaughter.

FRAU: For you, I'd break the law. Philip, we socialists have a big problem.

PHILIP: What? Socialism? I've been meaning to – [talk to you about that.]

FRAU: – Turkey! The one thing you know anything about. We want the Turks in. Socialists are not racists, we embrace Islam. But, look at Holland.

PHILIP: Kaw! What a cock up!

FRAU: When that madman killed Theo van Gogh, that was Europe's 9/11. Holland used to be a perfect illustration of liberal European values – tolerance –

PHILIP: – legal pot –

FRAU: – gay rights –

PHILIP: – great pornography –

FRAU: – freedom of speech –

PHILIP: – and a sex worker industry that was the envy of the world!

FRAU: – a live and let live culture. There was a time when a Muslim living in Holland didn't mind living next door to a live sex show –

PHILIP: – he either kept his head down, or joined in!

FRAU: Madrid, the 7/7 bombings – hell! We socialists are not Islamophobic, we're not against Turkey, but it's common sense. If Methodists were going around blowing themselves up, trying to kill us all, we'd think twice about letting the Welsh in wouldn't we.

PHILIP: They're in already, it's too late.

FRAU: We socialists publicly support Turkey's accession but privately we're –

PHILIP: – Bricking it?

FRAU: Apprehensive.

FRAU moves over to the side table and eyes up the twiglets. PHILIP seems powerless to do anything about it. Enter ANDRE who notices FRAU's interest in the twiglets.

Erdogan has scrapped adultery as a criminal offence – gut! – but virginity testing is still practised, and honour killings are rife.

PHILIP: You can lead a horse to water, but you can't make it windsurf.

FRAU: We Germans don't like metaphor. We don't see the point in beating around the bush.

ANDRE removes the twiglets from out of FRAU's reach. FRAU watches where they go.

ANDRE: (*To PHILIP.*) Whenever she rings, I have to put my tools back in the bag, and go home and fornicate!

PHILIP: Excuse me Andre, but I'm in a meeting now.

ANDRE puts the twiglets on a different side table and carries on with his work.

The plumber. He's trying for a baby with his girlfriend and so am I.

FRAU: With his girlfriend?

PHILIP: No, with my partner, Nicola.

FRAU: You and Nicola are not married?

PHILIP: No.

ANDRE: (*To FRAU.*) She's flying over today, to be serviced! We men are nothing to you women. We are the cheap form of IVF!

ANDRE goes into Bed 2.

PHILIP: I'm sorry about this.

FRAU: No, no! It is most apposite. In ten years Turkey will
have a population of over one hundred and fifteen million,
which would make them the most powerful nation in
the European Union. Imagine the Common Agricultural
Policy written by Muqtada al-Sadr.

PHILIP: It reads like a bad translation from the Arabic already.

FRAU: Yet the Islamification of Europe will bring many
advantages.

PHILIP: Will it?

FRAU: Yes. I'd like you to write a report –

PHILIP: – write a report? Oh no.

FRAU: It's called 'virk' Philip.

PHILIP: That word's always sounded a bit German to me.
What if I just tell you, now, what I think?

FRAU: You have ideas?

PHILIP: It's an idea of Sasha's that I thought of this morning.

SASHA looks over, and catches his eye.

As I see it religion is the key here.

FRAU: Are you religious Philip?

PHILIP: I'm not sure if God exists.

FRAU: Church of England then?

PHILIP: Yes.

*SASHA moves the twiglets. It now looks as if FRAU FLUGEL-
HAMMERLEIN is actively chasing them.*

If we socialists –

ANDRE: – (*To PHILIP.*) We play fantasy games. Lorry driver /
waitress. Pilot / air hostess. Magician / magician's assistant

35

– that's my favourite. It is the only way I can get an erection.

PHILIP: Look Andre! You were very good on the athlete's foot but I do not have erection problems, and if I did I wouldn't ring a plumber AND I'm in a meeting!

ANDRE slopes off into Bed 1.

FRAU: Belgian?

PHILIP: Yeah. Not even a good plumber. I've known serial killers use less duct tape. So, I propose a vote to censure the Commission for being out of touch with the people of Europe in agreeing to Turkish accession.

FRAU: The right-wingers in the Christian Democrats would support that.

PHILIP: Yes, but the democrat Democrats, the free marketeers, would oppose it.

FRAU: And the EPP slash ED split would fatally widen. Their alliance would be –

PHILIP: – Kaput!

FRAU: Tot!

PHILIP: Gesundheit!

FRAU: And we socialists would be left as the biggest grouping in the Parliament and could finally deliver a truly socialist Europe.

PHILIP: Yup!

FRAU: This censure could make your name Philip.

PHILIP: The Wardrobe Censure. But… Problem, I'm incredibly in bed with the Turks –

FRAU: – who do we know in the Christian Democrats? Beatrice Renard! My sources tell me that you're quite close to her.

PHILIP: I had an in depth meeting with her last night.

FRAU: You were dancing on the tables in Les Aviateurs. She in bra and knickers; you down to your underpants.

PHILIP: Boxer shorts. There's a world of difference.

FRAU: Set up a meeting with her today –

PHILIP: – not today! Today is about –

FRAU: – Philip! Why did you come into politics?

PHILIP: Because I like telling people what to do.

FRAU: (*With a bribing wink/equivalent.*) But are you ambitious? I will be making a Socialist nomination for President of the Parliament very soon.

PHILIP: Me? President of the European Parliament?

FRAU FLUGELHAMMERLEIN makes to leave. At the door she turns.

FRAU: I have underestimated you. But…for the Presidency you would need to be married.

FRAU leaves. PHILIP spins into action.

PHILIP: President! Ha, ha! Get Beatrice Renard on the phone!

SASHA: But I thought today was going to be about making babies.

PHILIP: We can get the politics done this morning and make babies this afternoon. Tell Beatrice I would love to have coffee with her, here, now.

SASHA: No! Mehmet will be here any minute. You don't want Beatrice throwing herself at you when Mehmet's here. How about Mehmet at nine, and Beatrice at ten?

PHILIP: That's exactly the solution I was going to suggest that you thought of.

SASHA: Can I remind you, the Parliament register will be open now?

PHILIP: I can't be arsed to sign today.

SASHA: (*Angry.*) Pederast! You earn a hundred and eighty euros just for signing your name! Some of my people in your country are picking tomatoes all week for less than what you get paid for two seconds work!

PHILIP: OK. OK. I'll go and sign. Back in a tick. And don't call me a pederast. I know it's a common Russian swear word but it's really not appropriate. Arsehole, twat, wanker – I wouldn't argue with any of those.

PHILIP leaves.

SASHA: (*On the phone.*) 'Allo.

ANDRE appears, checks out SASHA, and sits on the couch and lights a cigarette. SASHA watches him as he smokes and spreads out.

Je vous appelle de la part de Philip Wardrobe... Oui, Sasha, c'est moi...cela lui ferait plaisir de prendre un café avec vous ce matin...dix heures?...parfait. Ciao.

(*To ANDRE.*) It's no smoking in here.

ANDRE: We need to talk. (*He tears off his moustache. Muted.*) Ah!

SASHA: Is that a false moustache?

ANDRE: No. It is a real moustache which I tear off my face when I feel like a change. I am a master of disguise. They call me the 'Chameleon'. I created a plumbing problem in your room so that I could get access.

He shows her his ID.

You know what OLAF is I presume?

SASHA: It's the fraud investigation department of the Commission. Despite the fact that nine billion euros has gone missing, you have never successfully prosecuted anyone.

ANDRE: The longer an animal goes without killing and eating, the hungrier it gets.

SASHA: MEPs call you the Office for the Legalisation and Acceptance of Fraud. Why are you interested in me? I am a student.

ANDRE: Your student visa ran out on March the first this year.

SASHA: (*Genuinely distressed.*) Please don't deport me! I send my money home. My father can't work. He had an industrial accident when –

ANDRE: – It's not you we're after. OLAF is not the immigration service, although I can always make a phone call. Are you going to help me today?

SASHA: Do I have a choice?

ANDRE now goes around placing listening devices around the main room and in Bed 1.

ANDRE: Mr Wardrobe employs this Nicola Daws, his partner, as his full-time Office Manager in the UK. Pays her eighty thousand euros a year. However, Nicola Daws is the full-time Secretary General of Human Rights Now! I have a good nose for a bad stink.

SASHA: I'm not involved!

ANDRE: I understand there is not much in the way of employment in your home town of Murmansk. Fish processing.

SASHA: Suka! Tva-ya mama sa-syot sobachie khuy-ee!

ANDRE: I was not aware that my mother has sex with animals.

SASHA: You speak Russian?!

ANDRE: Chameleon and polyglot.

SASHA: I've never met Nicola. What are you doing?

ANDRE: This is an omni-directional condenser microphone.

SASHA: You can't do that, can you?

ANDRE: Do you wish to see the paperwork? This will be my office.

He goes into the linen cupboard and puts on headphones.

SASHA: So you're going to sit in that cupboard all day?

ANDRE: Yes. But the next time you see me I will be in disguise, and you will introduce me as the newly elected MEP for Malta.

ANDRE closes the cupboard door. Enter PHILIP, carrying a bouquet of roses.

PHILIP: I think I've shook the bastard off!

SASHA: Who?

PHILIP: Mr Fucking Clean. Hans Peter Martin. He was hiding in a rubber plant filming all the MEPs signing in and leaving straight away. Eight of us had to sneak out through the kitchens.

During the next PHILIP goes into Bed 1 and puts the flowers in a vase.

Is Madame Renard coming up then?

SASHA: Ten o'clock yes. Turkish ambassador at nine.

PHILIP: (*Off.*) Just time to do my expenses from yesterday.

SASHA: (*Looking to the cupboard.*) Expenses? NO! Now is not a good time to do expenses.

PHILIP: (*Returning.*) Any time is a good time to do expenses! Ching! Ching! Most important job of the day! Come on!

SASHA: (*Loud.*) OK! Yesterday. Travel! Brussels to Strasbourg. You shared a car so I'll claim twenty euros petrol money.

SASHA nods violently.

PHILIP: Are you mentally ill?! Yes, I shared a car, but we claim Air France club class return. Should be near enough fifteen hundred euros.

SASHA is mouthing 'No' and 'Shh!!'

What?! Hard earned money that. You want to try sitting in the kid's seat of a Renault Espace for five hours while six drunk Dutchmen run a sensationally well organised farting competition. Grandad Wardrobe was a miner, but he never had to work in those conditions. My canary committed suicide before we'd left Belgium.

Exits to Bed 1 looking for receipts. ANDRE comes out of the cupboard in disguise.

(*Returning.*) There's some more here. Tractor bar...thirty-seven fifty; Mickey Mouse bar...eighty-five ten; Kitty O'Shea's...two euros? That can't be right. How long have you been standing there?

ANDRE: We Maltese are used to being ignored.

SASHA: This is the, a, new MEP for Malta.

ANDRE: (*Offering hand.*) Louis Casa, Partit Nazzjonalista.

PHILIP: (*Half to SASHA.*) Do we have an appointment?

ANDRE: I saw Frau Flugelhammerlein this morning in the lobby. I am a Democrat, a Christian, and very unhappy with Turkey's accession.

PHILIP: I see! OK! Sasha – coffee please! I thought I'd met all five of the Maltese members.

ANDRE: I replace Richard Peralta. He said he could not afford to be an MEP for Malta and that he earned more smuggling finches.

PHILIP: Finch smuggling's big business in Malta is it?

ANDRE: Office cleaners in Brussels earn more than Maltese MEPs.

PHILIP: No?!

ANDRE: I am paid one thousand three hundred euros a month. An Italian MEP –

PHILIP: – ten times as much. I know, and do they ever turn up! Non mai!

(*Taking him aside.*) Look Louis, your best bet for steady cash is to employ your wife to run your office back in Malta.

SASHA is gesticulating.

ANDRE: My wife already has a job.

PHILIP: Is she in finches?

ANDRE: Finch smuggling is illegal.

PHILIP: You can claim twelve thousand euros a month for her! She doesn't have to do anything.

SASHA is gesticulating.

ANDRE: Is your wife working full time for you?

SASHA is miming digging, working hard, sweating brow, etc.

PHILIP: She works hard for me in short spells, and very very hard in longer spells at busy times. She works so hard she makes herself cry and is borderline suicidal.

SASHA mimes stress by pointing her index fingers to either side of her head.

She is asthmatic too, and nearly died once when she got an arrow through her head, when she was stressed!

ANDRE: And you split the money I suppose?

SASHA mimes 'a hole'.

PHILIP: Are you mad? If she digs the garden as well of course I pay her, a hole, she gets one hole, cash, ah yes! the whole of it! I don't take any of it. It's hers! After all, she dug the bloody thing!

SASHA gives up exhausted.

Rule number one with expenses, repeat after me, 'IF YOU'RE IN THE AIR, YOU'RE EARNING.'

ANDRE: (*Smug. To SASHA.*) If you're in the air, you're earning!

SASHA: (*Groaning.*)

ANDRE: Thank you for seeing me at such short notice

PHILIP: Don't you want to talk about the vote of censure?

ANDRE: You have my vote.

PHILIP: Thanks.

ANDRE leaves.

That went well. One democrat in the bag already. Only ninety-nine to go.

SASHA: I am going down to the lobby now to leave this bomb with reception.

SASHA leaves with the jiffy bag. PHILIP appears chuffed to be on his own and picks up the phone and dials a number.

PHILIP: (*On phone.*) Nicola, it's me…how about a bit of role play this afternoon?… Lorry driver / waitress?… Pilot / air hostess?… Magician / magician's assistant!?… Well what's your fantasy?… That's not going work is it!… Because I'm not in it! …President and whore?… Yeah! you speak French, can you do Parisian whore?… Great. See you later.

(*Off the phone.*) French whore! Ooh, yum, yum.

Phone down. Knock on the door. PHILIP opens it and EDDIE FREDERICKS enters. An MEP and Yorkshire pig farmer of about 55. There is a copy of the Daily Mail in his jacket pocket, visible. He wears a Remembrance Day poppy. He is carrying a brown briefcase and a sleeping bag.

EDDIE: How do?

PHILIP: You can't stay here Eddie!

EDDIE: – Yer not a man of yer word then?

PHILIP: Oh bugger. What did I say?

EDDIE: 'If yer bring me post up from Brussels yer can sleep on the floor.'

EDDIE hands over a pile of post in which there is a large jiffy bag.

PHILIP: And when did I make this astonishingly stupid offer?

EDDIE: British beer club, last orders, Thursday. Yer said I were the best bloke yer'd ever met and that you loved me.

PHILIP: And exactly how much had I had to drink?

EDDIE: Dunno, I can't count past ten. Kaw! I'm worn out. Three weeks in Brussels, and then every bloody fourth week pack up and off to Strasbourg. Barmy! Eleven billion quid for nowt. If you paid an architect to design you an 'ouse and he put the bedroom in Leeds and the bog in Scarborough you'd think he were mad wunt yer?!

PHILIP: The Brussels / Strasbourg thing is a symbol of the reconciliation between Germany and France.

EDDIE: If they want a symbol of reconciliation they can 'ave a framed photograph of my arse.

Enter SASHA with the day's newspapers.

SASHA: Hello Eddie.

EDDIE: Hello Sash love. Looking gorgeous!

PHILIP: Why don't you just pay for your own hotel and claim it back?

EDDIE: Cos as the UKIP MEP for the East Riding of God's Own Country I made a commitment that if I won a seat on this disgusting gravy train I would travel in the guards van.

(*He takes out a snap tin and a flask.*) What do you think?

PHILIP: What do I think about what?

EDDIE: Winston Churchill – cigar; Margaret Thatcher – 'andbag; Eddie Fredericks – snap tin and flask. Iconic symbols of thrift and incorruptibility.

PHILIP: Utter genius.

SASHA: I think the briefcase is too smart.

EDDIE: They're flogging them off in the lobby for ten euros a shot.

SASHA inspects the briefcase. She's impressed.

PHILIP: You can't stay here! The Turkish ambassador is due any moment and will be incredibly not impressed when he discovers that I spend my leisure time with a direct descendant of Cro Magnon Man.

SASHA: (*To EDDIE.*) Hang on! Eddie, you get on well with the British Tories don't you?

EDDIE: I wunt trust 'em as far as I could chuck 'em.

SASHA: What I mean is, on policy, you're close?

EDDIE: Only cos they nicked our policies.

SASHA: (*To PHILIP.*) There's twenty-seven British Tories, potentially that's twenty-seven anti-Turkish votes in the censure and they'll talk to Eddie, here, at lunchtime, if there's a free buffet.

PHILIP: Eddie! Let me show you to your room!

EDDIE: Champion! It's a bog I need! I've had a couple of prisoners due for parole since Luxembourg.

Leads him to Bed 1. EDDIE goes off into Bath 1 and PHILIP reappears holding jiffy bag.

PHILIP: This is the third incredibly brilliant idea of yours I've had today already. Ring all those Tories up, and invite them here for lunch.

SASHA: But what about Nicola? Today is about you and Nicola.

PHILIP: She doesn't get here until four. Lunch'll be over by then. (*Holding up jiffy bag.*) What's he doing with this?

SASHA: That's not ours. That's not our bomb.

PHILIP: No? OK.

PHILIP puts it down. He sits at the coffee table and picks up the newspaper. Enter ANDRE without knocking.

I thought you were done?

ANDRE opens the cupboard and goes in.

Does he know he's gone in the linen cupboard?

Linen cupboard door opens.

ANDRE: The stopcock is in here.

ANDRE closes the door.

PHILIP: (*Standing, holding the paper, reading.*) MEP IN TURKISH ORGASM STORM. Beatrice Renard, Chair of the Women's Committee, bla bla bla, said she won't vote to let Turkey into the EU until Turkish men learn to provide the thirty-six million women of that nation with the orgasms which are their right as citizens of a liberal democracy. Women's position in Islam, bla, bla, bla. OH BUGGER! Trust her!

SASHA: Hell hath no fury.

Toilet flush is heard.

PHILIP: Turkey is a secular democracy happily enjoying a sensationally brilliant eclectic mix of East and West. But all Madame Bloody Renard and the women's committee can get on the lens is thirty-six million non-occurring orgasms!

Enter EDDIE from Bed 1.

EDDIE: That's trap one out of action for ten minutes.

PHILIP: (*Looking at watch.*) Right, we spend half an hour tops with Mehmet and get him out the building sharpish cos if he bumps into Renard there'll be blood on the carpet, my blood!

EDDIE: Why do you want us out the road at four o'clock? Are you on a promise?

SASHA: Nicola's flying over.

EDDIE: Course! You're trying for a baby aren't you! Smashin'!

EDDIE sits down in front of the twiglets and eyes them up. SASHA moves them.

Who's the problem? You or her?

PHILIP: We're both fine, it's just one of those unutterably tedious modern city living overworked stressy things.

EDDIE: Sperm count.

PHILIP: Eddie, I am totally and utterly committed to ignoring you.

EDDIE: King Arthur, my Suffolk Old Spot boar, well, I was gerrin a lot of sows not in pig after service, so I took to packing his balls with ice.

PHILIP: We're a bit short of ice.

EDDIE: Sperm are like cod or haddock. They love the cawld.

PHILIP: Eddie. This morning I have a negotiation with the Turkish ambassador, and a meeting with Madame Renard, Chair of the European Parliament Women's Committee. Instinct alone tells me that I would not perform at my best in either of those delicate situations if I sat there with my testicles packed in ice.

EDDIE: This in't important, yer know – politics. Kids is the only job in the world any of us have to get right.

SASHA: It can't do any harm can it? Give it a go.

SASHA begins to prepare a beer mug style glass with ice.

EDDIE: Gerra glass of water, put some ice in and then whenever yer can, five minutes at a time, nip into the bog and just give 'em a little dip.

SASHA: Still or sparkling?

EDDIE: Personally I'd go for sparkling. And bung a slice of lemon in.

SASHA: What does the lemon do?

EDDIE: Nowt. Burr if yer drink it accidentally, it tastes better.

PHILIP: Does it work?

EDDIE: Every squirt'll have ten million swimmers.

SASHA stands before PHILIP with the glass.

SASHA: This is the last of the ice. That's your ration for the day.

PHILIP: (*To EDDIE.*) Little dip, whenever I can?

EDDIE nods. PHILIP takes the glass and goes into Bath 1 through Bed 1. EDDIE sits at the coffee table. There is a knock on the main door.

SASHA: (*Looking at watch.*) Mehmet!

SASHA panics and picks up the first copy of the Daily Mail.

No bin!

She opens the cupboard and ANDRE takes the paper. She then lets in the Turkish ambassador. He is a handsome man in a western suit, carrying a briefcase which is identical to EDDIE's. He obviously fancies himself a bit. He also carries SASHA's jiffy bag 'bomb'.

MEHMET: Bonjour mademoiselle.

SASHA: Good morning, Mr Aziz? I'm Sasha, Mr Wardrobe's stagiaire.

MEHMET: Enchanté.

SASHA: This is –

They shake hands.

EDDIE: – Eddie Fredericks. Yorkshireman, Pig Farmer, and UKIP member – in that order.

MEHMET: You are Yorkshire not English?

EDDIE: Forget yer Islam, forget yer Christianity – there's onny three sorts of folk in the world: Yorkshiremen, them as wanna be Yorkshiremen, and them what lacks ambition.

MEHMET: – Is Mr Wardrobe here?

SASHA: He's just having a little dip.

MEHMET: There is a pool? Mmm. It is a magnificent hotel. Very old Europe.

SASHA: Please sit down.

MEHMET and EDDIE sit at the coffee table. MEHMET seems to be nursing the briefcase and he puts it on his lap. EDDIE puts the twiglets on the table and takes the newspaper from his pocket and puts it on the table...

MEHMET: The receptionist asked me to give you this envelope.

EDDIE: So Mohammed, what do –

MEHMET: – Mehmet.

EDDIE: What do you think of the European Union then?

MEHMET: We Turks are very positive about Europe.

EDDIE: Gerr out while yer can son.

MEHMET: We're not even in yet.

EDDIE: That's the best time to gerr out.

MEHMET: Seventy-five percent of our population want us to join. It is a beautiful realisation of a desire for peace and harmony from a continent that has known terrible war. Through trade we make friends – do you make war with your friends? No. You mustn't forget that we have been in Nato for over fifty years.

EDDIE: (*Touches poppy.*) I an't forgorren Gallipoli.

MEHMET: We are a young nation, we look forwards.

EDDIE: So you're trying to get membership of an exclusive club when you hate the guts of one of the members.

MEHMET: Cyprus does not exist.

EDDIE: How are yer gonna trade with a nation what dun't exist then?

MEHMET: People like you, you have these 'objections' to Turkish membership, ha! they are a smoke-screen to hide your racism.

EDDIE: I'm not a racialist and I've got nowt against Muslins. If it weren't for them you cou'n't gerr a pint of milk on Christmas day.

MEHMET: What you think of the European Union?

EDDIE: It's a German / French stitch up. Ironically, we started it. After't second war Winston Churchill come ovver here and ses to 'em all – 'Look, we're pig sick of you lot falling out all the time and expecting us and the Yanks to sort it out, so why don't you start a club, we don't wanna join, but for Christ's sake just tell us the one phone number so we know who to call next time the shit hits the fan.'

SASHA snatches the twiglets away from MEHMET's grasp. PHILIP appears from door of Bed 1. In his hand he carries the glass of iced water, which he puts on the coffee table.

PHILIP: Mr Aziz! What a pleasure to see you again!

MEHMET: Good to see you.

PHILIP: Please sit down. Some coffee for Mr Aziz.

MEHMET: I'd prefer just a glass of water please.

PHILIP: A glass of water please Sasha!

SASHA prepares a glass of water for MEHMET and delivers to stage right on the coffee table.

PHILIP: – Eddie! Do you want to unpack? In 'your' room.

EDDIE: Unpack? What's that? Polite for bugger off?! Done.

EDDIE goes into Bed 1 and closes the door. PHILIP sits next to MEHMET, who shuffles along the sofa towards the medicinal water. PHILIP is now in front of MEHMET's water (no lemon) and MEHMET is in front of the medicinal water, with lemon. PHILIP drinks from the clean glass, but realises his mistake. MEHMET sees him take the drink and takes a hold of the medicinal water but doesn't drink. PHILIP is like a rabbit in the headlights.

MEHMET: Prime Minister Erdogan is concerned about the growing volume of anti-Turkish rhetoric.

PHILIP: Yeah?

MEHMET: We have met the Copenhagen criteria and yet there seems to be an endless procession of anti-Islamic speakers. Franz Fischler. He even suggests that Turks are Asian Orientals unable to understand a liberal tolerant Europe. These racist ideas should be being countered by you.

MEHMET pauses and raises his glass. PHILIP holds his arm.

PHILIP: Hang on! Sasha! Did you want lemon?

MEHMET: Yes, I like lemon, this is fine.

PHILIP: Sasha! Mr Aziz doesn't want lemon!

MEHMET: This is perfect, ice and lemon.

PHILIP: Oh my God! It's a hair! Look!

SASHA whips it away, and replaces it with a new glass – without lemon. SASHA puts the glass in the fridge.

Carry on, sorry!

MEHMET: Have you seen this?

He passes over a photocopy of a letter.

It's a memorandum from Human Rights Now! to Prime Minister Erdogan. This Nicola Daws –

PHILIP: – Nicola!

MEHMET: Do you know her?

PHILIP: Nicola Daws? Rings a bell.

MEHMET: She's the Secretary General of Human Rights Now!

PHILIP: Ah, yes, her, yes, she's –

MEHMET: – a real bitch. She has the cheek to suggest that our harmonisation laws are just a sop to the EU and that the Turkish police are still routinely torturing people with impunity. What are you going to do about that?

PHILIP: I'll sort her out later. This afternoon.

MEHMET: OK. Now. Money.

PHILIP: My second favourite word. Ha!

MEHMET: What's your favourite word?

PHILIP: Cash.

MEHMET: This is cash. (*Opens case.*) A million euros.

PHILIP: Wow! Really, you shouldn't have. It's a nice case too, isn't it?

MEHMET: Can she be trusted?

PHILIP: One step out of line and she's on the next train back to Murmansk.

PHILIP takes out a bundle and fondles the money, taking a rubber band off the wad.

MEHMET: It is an unofficial payment, understand? Don't bank it, just spend it.

PHILIP: Don't worry, you've chosen the right man, I know what to do, I've spent money before. Do you want the rubber bands back?

MEHMET: A million euros is only a gesture. When Turkey is eventually allowed in, my country will receive twenty-five billion euros a year in subsidies. But each year we sit in the waiting room –

PHILIP: – is another twenty-five billion you've lost?!

MEHMET: Exactly! I am proposing a deal this morning. We will pay you a bonus of a million euros for each year we don't have to wait.

PHILIP: So if Turkey got the green light next year, nine years earlier than you expect, my bonus would be nine million euros, but if it takes ten years I would get nothing?

MEHMET: Exactly.

PHILIP: For nine million euros I'll get you in the club even if you're wearing trainers.

They shake hands.

MEHMET: Excellent!

PHILIP: Twenty-five billion should sort out the Turkish debt mountain, eh?

MEHMET places his hand over PHILIP's mouth.

MEHMET: (*In a panic.*) Shhh!!! No one is allowed to say Turkish debt mountain!

PHILIP: You just said Turkish debt mountain.

MEHMET: Shh!!!! Those three words are now illegal under article 301 of the Turkish Penal Code.

PHILIP: I'm not Turkish.

MEHMET: You work for us!

PHILIP: What would happen to a Turk caught saying the words Turkish debt mountain?

MEHMET: Three years in prison. (*Standing, picking up the paper.*) What the hell is this!

PHILIP: What?

MEHMET: MEP in Turkish orgasm storm! What!?

PHILIP: You don't want to read that.

MEHMET: (*Reading.*) No! This is the sort of media coverage we pay you stop happening. Beatrice Renard. That crazy whore!

PHILIP: I didn't think it was too much to get excited about, I mean she's –

MEHMET: – it is unbelievable. Phil, I have to say, it is this kind of thing which makes us question how effective your consultancy work is for Turkey. I may have to take my case back with me.

PHILIP: What? No! I've worked tirelessly for Turkey. (*With a wink to SASHA.*) Only people who are effecting change, make enemies.

SASHA gives him the jiffy bag.

Oh no! Not another one!

MEHMET: What is it?

PHILIP: Another jiffy bag bomb.

They all stand. PHILIP leaves the letter bomb on the coffee table.

Don't panic Mehmet. I've had a few of these.

MEHMET: Really?

PHILIP: Oh yes, usually racists. When I started putting the case for Turkey, kaw!, that's when the hate mail started. Sasha, run a bath please.

SASHA goes into Bath 1 and starts to run a bath.

You have to isolate the bomb, submerge in water.

SASHA comes out of Bed 1.

SASHA: It's running.

PHILIP: (*To MEHMET.*) Excuse me.

PHILIP exits into Bed 1 / Bath 1 with the bomb. EDDIE comes out of Bed 1. SASHA picks up the phone and dials.

EDDIE: I'm not staying in there.

SASHA: (*On the phone.*) Allo! La police s'il vous plaît… Oui, c'est pour vous signaler que M Philippe Wardrobe a reçu un autre jiffy bag bomb… Oui, je sais que c'est étonnant, cela en fait trois… Merci, il n'a pas eu mal.

PHILIP reappears from Bed 1. There is a knock at the door. PHILIP opens the door. It is Madame BEATRICE RENARD. A fortyish, not unattractive French woman, well dressed in a rather downbeat way. PHILIP takes a look at her, and then slams the door and locks it.

PHILIP: For our own safety can I suggest we all go into Sasha's bedroom out of the way.

PHILIP pushes MEHMET, EDDIE, and SASHA into Bed 2.

That one is the biggest jiffy bag bomb we've had so far.

He then clicks the case of money closed and slings it into Bed 1. He then opens the main doors again and BEATRICE breezes past him, but looks about suspiciously.

BEATRICE: Bonjour Philip. Why did you slam the door in my face?

PHILIP: You're an hour early?!

BEATRICE: I know. I thought we could spend some more time together, after what you said last night.

PHILIP: I was drunk. Anyway you're a married woman.

BEATRICE pushes past him and gives him a big, lumpy jiffy bag.

BEATRICE: I have some post for you.

PHILIP: What the bloody hell is this?

BEATRICE: The boy on reception asked me to bring it up. I slept with your tie last night. We are both exhausted.

PHILIP: If it was that good – keep the tie! Look, I've got a proposal to make to you. Get in there. Quick!

BEATRICE: In the bedroom? For an English quickie!?

PHILIP: No, not that kind of proposal. I've got to talk to you about your party, the EPP. But not out here it's dangerous. This could be a letter bomb.

They go into Bed 1 and PHILIP rushes into Bath 1 and chucks the jiffy into the bath.

BEATRICE: OH!! I didn't realise you were important enough to get jiffy bag bombs. And look at you, you are so brave, so English.

PHILIP: I'll be with you in a minute. Stay in there!

PHILIP shuts the door to Bed 1 and opens the door to Bed 2. He is confronted by MEHMET. At that moment BEATRICE opens the door to Bed 1 and PHILIP slams the Bed 2 door shut.

BEATRICE: They are beautiful flowers Philip, and Chanel Number Five, and the card, well! What a message!

PHILIP: Shut that door!

She shuts the door. PHILIP sticks his head into Bed 2.

Sasha!

SASHA comes out.

Beatrice has turned up an hour early! Did Mehmet see her?!

SASHA: No. I didn't realise she was here!

PHILIP: We've got to get rid of Mehmet now, before they see each other. And! She thinks Nicola's flowers, and that furry fox message are for her.

SASHA: Beatrice Renard! 'Renard' is the French word for 'fox'. I get it! She thinks, you think, she is your furry fox. Agh!

PHILIP: Oh bugger! As I see it, I've got two options, I can either kill myself immediately and thereby avoid all future pain, or I can sit in the corner and rock catatonically. Which?! Advice please!

SASHA: Got it! Listen! I'll call the lift and hold it on this floor, doors open. Lock Renard in your room.

PHILIP: ...lock Renard in there...

SASHA: – then, when she's safely locked in, knock twice on my bedroom door.

PHILIP: ...my door, your door!

SASHA: – and then either me or Eddie, I'll tell Eddie the plan –

PHILIP: – tell Eddie –

SASHA: – one of us will run Mehmet straight out the doors into the lift, and out the building.

PHILIP: They mustn't see each other Sash!

SASHA goes out through the main doors and is seen calling the lift. PHILIP goes to Bed 2 door.

Eddie! A word!

Enter EDDIE from Bed 2.

EDDIE: What's gooin off?

PHILIP: The letter bomb's worked a treat, but if Mehmet sees Renard everything's off! And she's in there!

EDDIE: Oh bugger.

PHILIP: Tell Mehmet the police want the whole suite evacuated quickly but wait for me to knock twice on the door, cos I've got to get Renard locked in there first, somehow.

EDDIE: Jam a chair again' the 'andle.

PHILIP: Good.

EDDIE: So yer gonna knock twice?

PHILIP: Yeah.

EDDIE goes back into Bed 2. Enter BEATRICE from Bed 1.

BEATRICE: Philip, cheri.

PHILIP: Madame Renard! Get back in there!

BEATRICE: I cannot stay in here when there is a bomb!

PHILIP: The bomb is in the bath. It won't go off!

BEATRICE: Philip, the whole world knows me as the Chair of the Women's Committee, as a tough nutter –

PHILIP: – tough nut, but go on –

BEATRICE: – a feminist, but that does not mean that I do not feel.

PHILIP: You're a married woman. Jean-Claude.

BEATRICE: Ah, French men are dogs with no back legs. Always rubbing something against the floor. But I spent ten years in Basingstoke and I have had my eyes opened!

PHILIP: Was it just your eyes you had opened?

BEATRICE: English men 'ave a key for everything.

PHILIP: And what about Turkish men? You don't mind telling the world about them do you.

BEATRICE: Mehmet!? He has slept with forty-seven MEPs already. I was just another butterfly he pinned with his prick. I have had my revenge.

PHILIP: Tell me about it. Look! I prefer blondes, natural blondes or bottle blondes, it doesn't bother me if the collar and cuffs don't match. My girlfriend of ten years, Nicola, she's blonde. YOU'RE NOT MY TYPE OK!!

BEATRICE: – I could be blonde for you!

PHILIP: No! I wanted to see you to talk about a censure vote against the Commission on the Turkey accession.

BEATRICE: I will vote for that to please you.

PHILIP: I know but I need the votes of a hundred Christian Democrats.

BEATRICE: I can't tell them how to vote.

PHILIP: You could, especially the women. You're chair of the Women's Committee.

BEATRICE: I will get as many votes as you like if you do what you said you would do last night. Make love to me.

PHILIP: Stay in there!

He pushes her into Bed 1 and shuts the door. He jams a chair up against the door, but it is too big/or small. Bed 1 door opens and BEATRICE comes out.

BEATRICE: You can't push me about. Have you got another woman in here?

PHILIP: NO!

BEATRICE: I think you do.

She knocks on Bed 2 door twice. EDDIE comes out first and PHILIP sticks his head between BEATRICE's legs and hoists her onto his shoulders as EDDIE pulls down the film screen so that when MEHMET comes out he is looking at the screen and PHILIP's legs.

MEHMET: Goodbye Mr Wardrobe.

PHILIP: (*From behind the screen.*) Bye bye, Mehmet.

MEHMET: I really didn't realise that you had put yourself in personal danger in the service of the Turkish people.

PHILIP: (*From behind the screen.*) Oh you know, all in a day's work! See you!

MEHMET: I will tell Prime Minister Erdogan that in you he has chosen well. I would like to shake your hand to express my gratitude.

PHILIP comes out from behind the screen and shakes hands with MEHMET.

PHILIP: You must leave, the police are getting incredibly jumpy about the bombs.

MEHMET: Bombs? Plural?

PHILIP: Yes, I think we're up to three at the moment and counting.

MEHMET leaves. PHILIP closes the doors. PHILIP sends the screen back up, revealing BEATRICE balancing on the dado rail.

BEATRICE: Was that Mehmet?!

PHILIP: Yes!

BEATRICE: Cherie! You just saved my life!

PHILIP: I just saved my own life!

EDDIE: (*To BEATRICE.*) Are you chair of the Women's Committee?

BEATRICE: Oui.

EDDIE helps her down from the wall.

EDDIE: I gorra few good ideas you might be interested in.

BEATRICE: Some other time, monsieur, at the moment I am busy.

BEATRICE goes into Bed 1 and closes the door.

EDDIE: Wahey! You're in there kid!

PHILIP: I'd rather jump out of a plane wearing a parachute folded by Peter Mandelson.

EDDIE: It's worth the risk. For the votes. I can only deliver yer twenty-seven Tories.

PHILIP: (*Head in hands.*) Today was supposed to be about me, Nicola, and trying to make a baby. Simple, good, honest life. All of a sudden it's turned into a race for the Presidency, and the chance of picking up nine million euros!

EDDIE: Do what you like when you're President.

PHILIP: Oh God! I hadn't put the two together. If I become President, I can green-light Turkey, and pick up nine million. Have you ever seen a million, in cash?

EDDIE: I had a fifty pound note once.

PHILIP picks up the money case and is about to flick the catch when BEATRICE enters from Bed 1.

BEATRICE: Your furry fox is getting impatient.

She kisses him on the cheek. She's a little embarrassed.

I will wait in your chicken coup and try not to break the eggs.

BEATRICE exits to Bed 1.

EDDIE: Come on then. Let's have a butcher's!

PHILIP flicks up the lid.

Fuck me sideways!

A muffled mobile phone is heard.

PHILIP: Is that your mobile?

EDDIE: 'ant gorr a mobile.

PHILIP shuts the lid and picks up the jiffy back brought in by EDDIE and listens with his ear close up.

PHILIP: It's this one!

PHILIP rushes into Bed 2 and through into Bath 2. There is an explosion off.

To black.

End of Act One.

Act Two

Later that day at about 3:45. There are bottles of wine and the remnants of a buffet set out on one of the side tables. EDDIE is eating a ham sandwich from his snap tin. PHILIP is sitting on the sofa squinting. SASHA is dabbing his hands with TCP and applying elastoplasts. Both hands are amateurishly bandaged and occasionally he sticks a finger in his ear as if his hearing is affected. PHILIP's suit jacket is set on the back of a chair near the door.

SASHA: How do you feel now? (*Louder.*) How do you feel?

PHILIP: Someone somewhere wants me killed. I cannot tell you how sensationally happy this has made me! I feel important! Relevant! Effective! Why did you go into politics, Eddie?

EDDIE: I got to the top of the Young Farmers and there were nowhere else to go.

PHILIP: Westminster was so fantastically pointless. The only time I actually felt I'd achieved anything was 1997 when I managed to claim more expenses than Keith Vaz. This is my first taste of real politics and it is sensational! I love it. Ow!

SASHA: (*Momentarily stops dabbing his face/hands.*) – Sorry.

PHILIP: I want to be President of the European Parliament.

EDDIE: Aye, aye, I know you, you want the nine million an' all for shoeing in Turkey sooner rather than later.

PHILIP: It's not just the money. A modern, secular Turkey embraced by Europe would help to stifle terrorism.

EDDIE: Saving the world now are we?

PHILIP: Yes, actually. So Eddie, how many of those Tories we've just fed and Beaujolayed will be voting to censure the Commission on Turkey?

EDDIE: Don't believe worr anyone ses while yer feeding 'em!

PHILIP: Still, it's a another twenty-seven votes

SASHA: What are we going to do with the third jiffy bag? It might be another bomb.

EDDIE: Lightning don't strike twice.

EDDIE heads off for the bathroom of Bed 1.

SASHA: Is your vision normal?

PHILIP: My vision is normal IF at this moment we are in a discotheque half-way through an indoor fireworks display.

SASHA: You should go to the hospital.

Enter EDDIE carrying wet jiffy bag, which he has half opened already. SASHA hides at the back of the room and PHILIP covers his face with a cushion from the sofa. EDDIE looks into the envelope.

EDDIE: It's not a bomb. It's summat much worse than that.

He takes out a vibrator.

SASHA: (*To PHILIP.*) Have you been shopping on the internet?

Takes out sex play handcuffs.

EDDIE: One set of handcuffs, and one prick. It's a start-your-own police force kit. (*Producing a wet letter. He reads.*) Dear Mr Wardrobe MEP, I purchased this 'vibrator' for my wife to commemorate the sixtieth anniversary of VE day. As an electrical engineer I can say that the wattage ratio of the electric motor is inadequately torqued to drive the action of the head during normal use. Also, my wife, who is a health and safety officer, tells me that the fluffy bits of the handcuffs are not made from flame-retardant material, which could be dangerous because we're on gas. I have never found it easy to return faulty sex toys, but Tommy Jeffers, the landlord of the Cricketers in Oundle, told me that you are my local member for the European Parliament –

PHILIP: (*To SASHA.*) – take Jeffers off the Christmas card list.

EDDIE: – I would like you to pursue this issue in the European Court of Human Rights. Yours sincerely Abbas Ali Belhadj.

PHILIP: Where's he live?

EDDIE: Thrapston Village.

PHILIP: It's those pissheads in the Cricketers!

EDDIE: Maybe it's the lads in the Cricketers who sent the letter bomb an' all.

PHILIP: Na! The bomb will have been IslamoPHOBES, IslamoPHILES, or IslamISTS. One or the other, or all three working together. Or some Austrian racist Christian Democrat nutters club, or a lone Walloon loon.

EDDIE: What yer saying is yer an't gorr a clue?

PHILIP: A clue is exactly what I've not got. Who would you blame Eddie?

EDDIE: Gyppos.

SASHA: Eddie!

EDDIE: I'm a farmer, I blame Gyppos for everything.

She whacks him on the head, in a friendly manner.

PHILIP: The Romany Peoples are a significant racial minority with an amazingly rich culture.

EDDIE: Since when has nicking fences and eating hedgehogs been culture?

PHILIP: And what exactly is UKIP policy on the Romany Peoples? Is it in a document called 'The Final Solution'?

SASHA: That's shut you up Eddie.

EDDIE: No, I'm unshutupable. Any road it's time for another dip! Come on! I'll mix you another glass with ice?

SASHA: The old one's in the fridge – I said I'm short of ice.

EDDIE opens the fridge and takes out the glass.

EDDIE: Come on son, one last time! Cawld bath for Cannon and Ball!

Knock at the door. SASHA opens it. It's ANDRE, in a cheapish suit.

ANDRE: Bonjour.

PHILIP: Louis Caza. Malta. Are you still here? Do you want a drink?

ANDRE: (*To SASHA.*) Have you not told him?

SASHA: No.

ANDRE: I work for OLAF.

SASHA: He's a bit deaf.

ANDRE: I WORK FOR THE FRAUD INVESTIGATION TEAM OF THE PARLIAMENT.

PHILIP: I claim only my legal entitlement of expenses. This is an outrage! You can't – [come in here and masquerade…]

ANDRE: Calm down! I am no longer interested in you Mr Wardrobe. I 'ave a bigger fish on my 'ook. Beatrice is registered in the Parliament files as a married woman, and yet she told you this morning that she was single.

PHILIP: She might be lying. She's –

ANDRE: – She has an obsession with you obviously. I heard. I have sat in the linen cupboard all morning listening to you on the headphones.

PHILIP: (*Standing.*) You can't bug the rooms!

ANDRE produces a requisition. PHILIP looks at it with some difficulty.

ANDRE: Get her back here and I can record some pillow talk, maybe.

PHILIP: No way! It would be incredibly not in my interests for you to arrest Beatrice since she has a key role in my plans to be President.

ANDRE: In that case I will have this illegal alien deported back to Murmansk where the only employment is working as a whore on the brothel ship which services the Russian fishing fleet.

PHILIP: Go on then. Highly intelligent and attractive Eastern European interns are ten a penny.

SASHA: (*To PHILIP.*) Sooka! Yob tvoiu mat! Poshol na khui! Da chob thee vsu zizn el govno, nedonosok!

(*To ANDRE.*) Translate please.

ANDRE: I did not pick up the verb, but the nouns were 'her dog', 'your sister' and 'your mother's grave'.

PHILIP: (*To ANDRE.*) What do you want me to do again?

ANDRE: Invite Madame Renard back in here and get her to talk about her husband.

PHILIP: OK I get Renard back in here, you get your information, BUT you don't arrest her until after the vote tomorrow.

ANDRE: You are a proper politician aren't you?

PHILIP: I must be. I've had three letter bombs already today and we haven't had the second post yet.

ANDRE heads for the linen cupboard.

ANDRE: It's a deal. I will go back in here with the linen.

He goes in and shuts the door.

EDDIE: I think you've done quite well out of that. You were gonna see Madame Renard later on any-road weren't you?

PHILIP: Yes, I was, but in a safe place, a café, a public place. Somewhere not normally equipped with double beds, bidets, or baby oil.

EDDIE: I think you should take her up on her offer.

SASHA: And what is her offer?

PHILIP: 'I will get you as many votes as you like if you make love to me.'

SASHA: (*Amazed.*) NO!

PHILIP: She's nuts about me, I mean that is understandable, but I'm not going to actually ever sleep with her. Get her back in here right away. I want it over and done with before Nicola turns up.

PHILIP stands, picks up iced glass, and starts to head for Bed 1. SASHA gets on the phone.

SASHA: (*On the phone.*) 'Allo?…Madame Renard?… C'est encore moi, Sasha. Monsieur Wardrobe se demande s'il peut changer son rendez-vous avec vous. Toute de suite! Très bien, à bientôt.

EDDIE: How much was these bottles of wine?

SASHA: Seventy euros.

EDDIE: Fifty quid. Not bad for a case.

SASHA: Seventy euros each.

EDDIE: Fifty quid a bottle! Bloody hell. There's a bit left in the bottom of this one.

EDDIE pours himself a glass of wine.

SASHA: Excuse me, Mr Incorruptible.

EDDIE: (*He drinks.*) Aye. Mmm. There is a difference in't there. Between yer five quid Tesco's Frascati and yer fifty quidder.

There is a knock on the door. EDDIE opens it. It is a bespectacled
GENDARME, in a smart rather correct plain clothes suit.

GENDARME: Bonjour Monsieur! Je m'appelle Popineau,
Sécurité Nationale. Il pourait qu'il y a eu une petite bombe
ce matin. Est-ce que vous etiez ici a l'exact moment de
l'explosion?

EDDIE: Look son, I'm a great believer in supporting minority
and dying languages like French burr I don't speak it
mesen.

GENDARME: You speak English?

EDDIE: No. Yorkshire. It's a lot like English, but there's norr as
many words. Burr if we ever do say owt, we fucking mean
it.

GENDARME: You 'ave 'ad a small bom'?

EDDIE: Thank you. I used to do a lot of cycling. Now, do you
want a glass of wine?

GENDARME: Zank you.

EDDIE pours a glass of wine for the GENDARME and one for
himself. The GENDARME drinks.

EDDIE: Châteauneuf de summat or other.

GENDARME: – Pape.

EDDIE: Oh, I thought it were quite good mesen.

GENDARME: I am in a chamber up a rear passage of ze hotel.
I have a need to probe everyone who was in ze room.
Names! S'il vous plait?

SASHA: Mr Mehmet Aziz, Beatrice Renard, me, that's
Alexandria Togushev call me Sasha, Mr Edward Fredericks –

EDDIE: Eddie.

SASHA: – Mr Philip Wardrobe, and this man, I don't know his
name.

SASHA opens the cupboard door.

GENDARME: Why are you hiding in ze cupboard?

ANDRE: I'm not hiding. They know I'm here.

Beat. ANDRE shows him his ID card.

GENDARME: OLAF!

ANDRE: D'accord!

GENDARME: D'accord! Continuez.

Enter PHILIP, with glass in hand from Bed 1, not noticing the GENDARME.

PHILIP: I think it's actually incredibly working. But I want to squeeze one more dip in just before Nicola gets here OK, so I'm putting the glass back in the fridge OK to keep cool, because SHE won't let me have any of her precious ice OK. Brilliant Eddie! My testicles feel amazing! Hello. Who are you?

GENDARME: Inspecteur Popineau. I am ze chef here now. No one 'as permission to leave ze room unless zey are asking me for permissions first. I will probe you all. First, Monsieur Philip Wardrobe.

PHILIP: That's me. Good afternoon.

EDDIE: Can I nip down to the Parliament please? I've gorr all of this week's voting slips to tear up.

GENDARME: Five minutes, OK, but you do go inside ze Parliament chambers.

EDDIE: I wan't gonna. I did it once. I'd rather have someone brek coal on me head.

GENDARME: (*To SASHA.*) Mademoiselle, zis Beatrice Renard, when is she arriving?

SASHA: (*Checking her watch.*) In fifteen minutes.

GENDARME: Bien! Keep her here. She must not leave zis room. And ze Turk, ring him up and get him to come back 'ere for 'is deep probing.

PHILIP puts his suit jacket on.

GENDARME: Mr Wardrobe? Zis way please.

PHILIP and the GENDARME start to leave.

PHILIP: (*Close to panic.*) Nicola will want a bath. But for God's sake don't let her bump into – [bloody Renard, it –]

SASHA: – Phil! Nicola's not due for another hour.

PHILIP: Fine, but can you sort that bedroom too please.

PHILIP and the GENDARME leave. SASHA goes into Bed 1 and tidies up cursorily. EDDIE finishes off his glass of wine.

SASHA: What does Nicola look like, I've never met her. Or Renard either.

EDDIE: Didn't you see Renard this morning?

SASHA: No, I was in there, and then –

EDDIE: Nicola's blonde and English, and Renard's brunette and French. Righteo! I'm offski.

EDDIE leaves. SASHA is seen to be tidying up/making the bed etc. ANDRE comes out of the cupboard and surreptitiously pours himself a glass of wine before returning with a glass to the cupboard and closing the door. There is a knock at the door. SASHA comes out of Bed 1 and looks at her watch.

SASHA: (*Looking at her watch.*) Tvoiu mat!! This Renard woman is really crazy about him. Fifteen minutes early!

SASHA opens the door. It's NICOLA. She has a small valise with her. Her new hairstyle is short, brunette.

Bonjour madame. Vous êtes en avance!

NICOLA: Bonjour. Sasha?

SASHA: Oui, c'est moi. Entrez! Allez à côté!

SASHA pushes NICOLA towards Bed 2.

NICOLA: Ou est Philip?

SASHA: Il parle de la lettre piégée aux gendarmes. Il a un rendez-vous avec le –

NICOLA: – Est-ce que vous préférez parler en anglais?

SASHA: Sorry, yes I forgot, of course you speak perfect English don't you! From all that time you spent in Basingstoke.

NICOLA: I've been to Basingstoke, yes, but I don't remember learning anything. Phil told me about the letter bomb, is he alright?

SASHA: Yes, yes, it's nothing really. Actually the gendarme wants to talk to you.

NICOLA: And in what way am I involved?

SASHA: You were in this room when the bomb went off…

NICOLA: I'm sorry I was not in this room when the bomb went off. I was –

SASHA: – No! You weren't were you. You were – [in there.]

NICOLA's mobile phone goes off. She answers it.

NICOLA: Excuse me.

(*On the phone.*) Claude, how are you?… Good, well done… I'm in Strasbourg now and once I've got the Women's Committee up to speed we can run it past the Turks…let's embargo it until tomorrow…Ciao!

Turns off phone.

SASHA: I think your Women's Committee could do more for –

NICOLA: – Sasha sorry, it's not my Women's Committee AND I've just given myself the afternoon off, thank you.

SASHA: You're in here. Come on.

She closes the door on NICOLA in Bed 2. There is a knock at the door.

(*Looks at her watch.*) Who's this? Bliat!! It must be Nicola! If these two meet!

SASHA opens the main doors and we see BEATRICE standing there in new clothes and with a new blonde hair-do. At that moment NICOLA opens the door to Bed 2 and comes out. SASHA closes the door in BEATRICE's face.

NICOLA: Sasha, there's another woman's clothes in there.

SASHA: Yes. It's my room.

NICOLA: But what's wrong with Phil's room?

SASHA: Er… It's a crime scene. The police said.

NICOLA: Oh OK, because of the letter bomb?

SASHA: Yes.

NICOLA: And you don't mind me being in your room?

SASHA: No.

NICOLA: Thank you. That's very kind of you.

NICOLA goes back into Bed 2.

SASHA: (*Under her breath.*) Whore.

SASHA jams a chair up against the handle of Bed 2 then unlocks the main doors and opens them and lets in BEATRICE who this time breezes past her.

Hi! Nice to meet you at last!

BEATRICE: Hello. Sasha isn't it? Can you send an email to my office to let them know where I am. I'm expecting a phone call from the London office of Human Rights Now! and I don't want to miss it. You have my email address don't you?

SASHA: Yes. You know, I think the kind of work you do is just so important, I mean –

BEATRICE: – can you do that now? Please. It's important. I had my mobile phone stolen last night.

SASHA: No problem, whatever you want, just ask. You're in here, the master suite, Phil suggested I run you a bath.

SASHA goes into Bath 1 and starts running a bath.

BEATRICE: He wants me to have a bath? Well, well.

SASHA: He's crazy about you!

BEATRICE: Did he say that?

SASHA: You don't have a suitcase? Of course! You're not staying the night. What's that? Chanel number 5!

BEATRICE: Yes, it's Philip's favourite isn't it?

SASHA: Only because it's your favourite.

BEATRICE: Has Philip told you why I'm here?

SASHA: Yes! Don't be embarrassed! My Aunt Irena wanted a son, but my Uncle Sergei is impotent so Uncle Alexander stepped in, do you understand? They have five daughters and they're still trying. Ha! Sex is a functional thing. Phil is with the gendarme at the moment. We had a jiffy bag bomb this morning and –

BEATRICE: – I know.

SASHA: He told you about it did he? OK. We've called a doctor for Phil. He got you some flowers.

BEATRICE: Yes, I've seen the flowers. Sasha, would you please send that email.

SASHA: Yes, of course. Have a nice long soak.

She shuts the door behind her, and takes the chair from Bed 2 door and jams it against the handle of Bed 1. She then goes to the linen cupboard and opens it.

SASHA: (*Indicating Bed 2.*) What's she doing in there?

ANDRE: You know you've made a mistake –

The door to Bed 2 opens and SASHA closes the linen cupboard door quickly. NICOLA is wearing a dressing gown and carrying her Blackberry. She goes straight to the fridge and pours herself a glass of white wine from an open bottle.

NICOLA: Do you have any ice?

SASHA: No.

NICOLA: That's a serious problem then Sasha.

SASHA: Why?

NICOLA: I'm a modern working woman. I can't relax unless my body mass is at least eighty-seven percent white wine spritzer.

SASHA: We don't have any ice to spare and there's no soda water.

NICOLA: We seem to have got off on the wrong foot. I've had a very stressful morning, and I like a bath and a glass of fizzy, that's all!

SASHA: There's no point in you having a bath! He's not going to go through with it. I don't think it's decent, what you're doing!

NICOLA: Oh for fuck's sake! Do we have to be married or something? I'm forty-two. I've got to make the most of my opportunities.

NICOLA makes her way to Bed 2 with just a glass of wine.

I'll be in the bath.

NICOLA shuts the door of Bed 2. Enter PHILIP through main entrance doors.

SASHA: Nicola's here! She's in there.

PHILIP: What! She's an hour early.

SASHA: The bad news is Renard is here too.

PHILIP: Oh no! Oh no, oh no, no, no, please God, no. Bugger! Sasha, look, I'll pay you to kill me. I'll lie on the floor, you get a sharp pencil and stick it in my eye and then bang it in with a heavy book. Shit!! Where's Renard?

SASHA: Here, in my room.

PHILIP: So Nicola's in here?

PHILIP knocks on Bed 1 and goes in.

Darling?!

He comes out again.

She's in the bath. You've got to go and see the gendarme. Go on! I'll police these two. Room five-o-ten.

SASHA leaves. PHILIP opens the cupboard.

What's Beatrice doing in there?

ANDRE: They are both having baths. It's not an issue for me, but –

PHILIP: – Why is Renard having a bath? That is incredibly not good news.

ANDRE: She must be serious about this sex for votes thing. Looks like I will get my pillow talk.

PHILIP: And I'll get the clap! She's slept with Mehmet Aziz, don't forget, who's slept with forty-seven MEPs, mostly women, but not exclusively. But if they're both having baths that gives us a bit of breathing space.

ANDRE: I think –

PHILIP closes the door on ANDRE. Enter EDDIE through main doors. PHILIP assesses the situation and looks at his watch.

Eddie! Got a little job for you.

EDDIE: An't you gorra go see the doctor?

PHILIP: Yes, exactly, but we've got a tricky situation here. Nicola...

NICOLA comes out of Bed 2 unseen. She's wearing a towel. She's not yet got in the bath. PHILIP approaches Bed 1.

...is in here having a bath, and –

PHILIP notices NICOLA.

– Nicola! Bloody hell! Your hair! You look gorgeous!

They kiss. It's a real hug and kiss. EDDIE goes over and pours himself a glass of Pape.

NICOLA: Do you like it?

PHILIP: You look great!

NICOLA: I was worried, I know how much you need me to be blonde.

PHILIP: I've got photos if I need them, in an emergency.

NICOLA: (*Taking him aside.*) What the fuck is going on? The place is swarming with people. I've flown over here today to try for a baby, but it looks like you've been selling tickets to a live sex show.

PHILIP: Listen, it's complicated –

NICOLA: – there's nothing at all complicated about it. I've just taken a reading.

PHILIP: The thermometer's looking good yeah?

NICOLA: The reading said, 'Fuck now, lady, your eggs are dropping.'

PHILIP: Alright, I'm ready, nearly – you're not very French whore.

NICOLA: You're not very 'President'.

PHILIP: I'm a lot more 'President' than you would imagine actually.

NICOLA: I've got fish net stockings in my case.

PHILIP: Mmm nice. It's the accent I like. Toutes directions / autres directions; pas de pêcher; ou se trouve la toilette? – you know what I mean.

NICOLA: (*Cod French.*) Oh ma chérie, je ressens une douleur dans mon coeur.

PHILIP: Kaw!

They kiss. EDDIE coughs.

This is Eddie Fredericks…

NICOLA: UKIP Eddie Fredericks?

EDDIE: Guilty as charged.

NICOLA: I wrote to you about the comments you made about Travellers in the Daily Mail. I didn't get a reply.

EDDIE: I got your letter and purr it in me caravan, which is my office, intending to read it next morning, but that night a coupla gyppos pulled up in a transit and nicked the caravan.

NICOLA: I don't believe you.

EDDIE: They're the best distraction burglars in the business. They could nick the gold out of your teeth and you wouldn't notice, you'd be fascinated by some deliberately staged peripheral activity.

NICOLA: Do you employ your wife to run your UK office?

PHILIP: Not that again! Not now!

EDDIE: She's gorr enough on her plate running a pig farm. Has he got you doing that then?

NICOLA: I don't do anything.

PHILIP: (*Conscious of ANDRE in the cupboard.*) Shh!

NICOLA: It's immoral, claiming eighty thousand euros for me when I do bugger all.

PHILIP: Oh God. Shut up!

NICOLA: What happened to you?

PHILIP: Someone sent me a letter bomb and –

NICOLA: – Why you? I mean, with respect, you're a political nobody.

PHILIP: Actually, I am going to be the next future incoming incumbent President of the European Parliament.

NICOLA: President?! You!?

PHILIP: You're gonna be making love to the most powerful man in Europe. Is that a turn-on, or is that a turn-on?! I was hoping it could knock half an hour off the foreplay.

NICOLA: I can't make love in that room. You said there was a view, and a jacuzzi. All I can see out the window is a skip, and the kitchen bins.

She heads to Bed 1. PHILIP stands in front of the door. NICOLA puts her ear against the wall.

PHILIP: This is our room but it's a crime scene. There's a policewoman from forensics in there.

NICOLA: Having a bath?

NICOLA prowls the room looking for evidence of infidelity.

PHILIP: She's doing a reconstruction. I was just about to throw the bomb into a full bath of water when it went off.

NICOLA gives him what must be a familiar quizzical stare.

Don't look at me like that! I'm not having an affair!

NICOLA finds the vibrator.

NICOLA: (*Holding up the vibrator.*) And this belongs to the maid?!

PHILIP: One of my constituents sent me it in the post.

NICOLA: You're up to something Phil. Get rid of these people, go and see your doctor, then we'll try and make a baby.

She takes her wine from EDDIE and goes back into Bed 2.

PHILIP: Sasha thinks Renard is Nicola!

EDDIE: Leave it with me son. Come on, let's get you to that doctor.

EDDIE opens the main doors, leaves them open, and calls the lift, then he comes back into the main room, having left the main doors open.

PHILIP: How are we gonna keep them apart?

EDDIE: I'm gonna tell Renard that she's next for the gendarme interview and he wants her to wait outside his room.

PHILIP: You're brilliant Eddie.

EDDIE walks out of sight down the corridor with the chair. PHILIP shouts after him.

You're the best mate I've got over here Eddie. I'm sorry I said those things about you in the Guardian.

EDDIE: That dint even prick the skin kid. All my life I've had people coming up to me and saying 'you smell of pig muck'. That's what hurts. If yer wanna get me really upset, four words – 'you smell of pigs'.

EDDIE closes the lift doors and then the suite doors. He pours himself another glass of wine and sups it. Then he knocks on the door of Bed 1 whilst still holding on to the handle. BEATRICE opens the door. She is half-undressed.

The gendarme wants to interview you. Down the corridor, but there's a photographer from Paris Match in that bedroom waiting to take a snapshot of the Chair of the Women's Committee, half-naked in a Socialist MEP's bedroom.

BEATRICE: Merde!

EDDIE: (*Going into Bed 1.*) I've gorr a plan to get you out the room without being seen. And Andre in the cupboard, if yer listening, you'd better help out too.

BEATRICE lets him in. NICOLA comes out. She walks around the room. She listens at the door to Bed 1. The noise of a key in a lock is heard. NICOLA is confused as to where it comes from. She walks over to the cupboard and tries the door but it is locked. EDDIE comes out of Bed 1 and opens the main doors and goes out into the corridor and returns pushing a large chamber maid's linen trolley on wheels.

NICOLA: What are you doing?

EDDIE: Just helping out. Can't help gerrin' involved me. Nice bath?

NICOLA: Yes, thanks.

NICOLA goes back into Bed 2 closing the door behind her. EDDIE pushes the trolley close to the doors of Bed 1. The same noise of a key in the lock. EDDIE opens the cupboard door very slightly, hardly noticeable. EDDIE knocks twice on the door to Bed 1 and opens it himself. BEATRICE cannot be seen in Bed 1. NICOLA comes out of Bed 2 quickly expecting to see someone. She is suspicious. EDDIE is pushing the trolley towards the main doors.

Stop right there! OK! Let's see what she looks like!

NICOLA goes over to the trolley and slowly lifts the lid and looks in. BEATRICE sprints out of Bed 1 carrying her high heels, fully clothed, and hides in the cupboard, but without closing the door. NICOLA turns and then goes into Bed 1 to have a look. EDDIE coughs loudly, opens the main doors and BEATRICE sprints out of the cupboard and out through the main doors. EDDIE closes the main doors simultaneously with ANDRE closing the cupboard door. The sound of a key in a lock. NICOLA reappears, sees nothing. She goes over to the cupboard and tries the door but finds it locked. EDDIE pours a glass of wine for himself and one for NICOLA which he offers her. She takes it.

EDDIE: Why don't you move in there? It's a much nicer room.

NICOLA: I think I will.

NICOLA goes into Bed 2 and picks up her things and moves into Bed 1 leaving the door open. We see her enjoying the view of the Parliament. EDDIE picks up a bottle and rather groggily moves to Bed 2 and closes the door...

EDDIE: I'm gonna gerr a bit of shut-eye in here.

EDDIE goes into Bed 2 and closes the door. Enter SASHA; she sees NICOLA.

SASHA: What are you doing in there?! Get out!

NICOLA comes out of Bed 1.

NICOLA: Nice flowers.

SASHA: They're for his girlfriend.

NICOLA: (*Sits, genuinely shocked.*) Really.

SASHA: Yes, an English woman. He's known her for ten years.

NICOLA: I didn't expect her to be English. I thought some attractive stagiaire maybe, but – is she young?

SASHA: No. She's your age.

NICOLA: Hell, it would be easier to understand if she was young.

SASHA: Age is not the issue. Love, commitment and children, that's what it's all about.

NICOLA: Children?!

SASHA: Yes! They're going to get married and have children.

NICOLA: That's it. I'm going. You can tell him it's all off.

NICOLA takes her bags and goes out through the main doors and is seen pressing the lift buttons.

SASHA: That will give me pleasure!

SASHA closes the doors. She then pours herself a drink and slugs it down. The main doors open and BEATRICE enters hiding behind the chamber maid's trolley which she pushes to the door of Bed 1. SASHA sees her and BEATRICE realises she's been seen.

Why are you hiding?

BEATRICE: I am trying to avoid that photographer from Paris Match.

SASHA: There is no photographer from Paris Match.

BEATRICE: Eddie said there was a photographer.

BEATRICE makes her way to Bed 1 still hiding.

When Phil suggested we get together this afternoon I thought we would be alone.

SASHA: You mustn't be embarrassed! This is so important! It is the right time of the month for you, isn't it?!

BEATRICE: It's not the wrong time of the month.

SASHA: Then you simply must have sex!

BEATRICE: I like you, I like your attitude. I don't know how much Philip pays you but if ever you feel like a change, just give me a call.

SASHA: I'd really like to work for Human Rights Now! and –

BEATRICE: – I couldn't help you with that, but I have business ventures of my own which always need entrepreneurs, risk takers. You like money?

BEATRICE starts to undress revealing expensive lingerie.

SASHA: I send most of my money home. My mother is a lorry driver and my father is sick, but he still has to work. He assembles sunglasses on the kitchen table, and earns a few roubles. I want to buy them both a home in the country so they can retire.

BEATRICE: Tell Philip I'm ready.

BEATRICE gets into bed. SASHA closes the door. Enter PHILIP wearing bandages on both hands and bandages around his eyes and ears. A doctor is with him.

PHILIP: ARE YOU HERE SASHA?

DOCTOR: Bonjour. Are you Sasha?

SASHA: Yes, hi.

DOCTOR: I'm the doctor on call, it looks worse than it is, ha! All the bandaging is really preventative. The eyes are not damaged but they need a chance to rest, so ideally he should keep the pads on overnight and I will see him tomorrow. Sit down here Monsieur Wardrobe. (*Quite loud.*) This is the sofa!

PHILIP feels the back of the sofa.

PHILIP: (*Too loud.*) IS THIS THE SOFA?

DOCTOR: He's a bit deaf because I've applied soothing ear drops to both ears.

PHILIP: WHERE'S NICOLA?

SASHA: SHE'S WAITING FOR YOU IN THE MASTER BEDROOM!

(*To DOCTOR.*) Is he allowed to get excited?

DOCTOR: The eyes and ears need resting. Otherwise he's perfectly healthy. Now, I charge the hotel who charge the room and they require a signature and Monsieur cannot sign because he cannot read it and –

SASHA guides PHILIP onto the sofa.

SASHA: – You want me to come down and sign your contract?

DOCTOR: Not my contract, the hotel's.

Enter EDDIE.

EDDIE: Bugger me, it's the invisible man. Alright?

SASHA: He's a bit deaf Eddie. I'll come down in the lift with you. You're in charge Eddie. Renard's gone, so we can all relax. Nicola's in there, ready.

SASHA exits with the doctor. EDDIE picks up the vibrator and inspects it. He sits next to PHILIP on the sofa. He places the vibrator in his groin as if it were an erection.

EDDIE: Do you mind me doing this? DO YOU MIND ME DOING THIS?

PHILIP: NO. (*Beat.*) BUT THEN AGAIN I DON'T KNOW WHAT YOU'RE DOING.

EDDIE: I've always liked you Phil.

Mischievously and deliberately EDDIE takes PHILIP's hand and places it on the vibrator.

PHILIP: EDDIE!

EDDIE: It's the vibrator!

PHILIP: DON'T DO THAT! IS NICOLA IN THE BEDROOM?

EDDIE: AYE! ARE YER READY?!

PHILIP: YEAH, READY!

EDDIE: That's my boy! I'LL TEK YER THROUGH. COME ON.

EDDIE gets up and puts the vibrator back on SASHA's desk then pulls on PHILIP's arm.

PHILIP: SASHA GOT THEM MIXED UP EARLIER. HAVE YOU SORTED IT OUT?

EDDIE: I PUT NICOLA IN THE MASTER BEDROOM MESEN! AND RENARD IS WITH THE COPPER DOWN THE CORRIDOR.

PHILIP: WHAT DID YOU SAY!?

EDDIE: IT'S ALL SORTED!!

EDDIE leads him to Bed 1 and knocks on the door.

EDDIE: Hello love. You've gorr a visitor!!

BEATRICE: (*Off.*) Je suis toute nue!

Door is closed.

EDDIE: That's funny she's speaking French. I SAID SHE'S TALKING FRENCH! JE SUIS TOUTE NUE. WHAT DOES THAT MEAN?

PHILIP: Perfect! She says she's naked.

EDDIE: Crikey!

PHILIP: Nicola said she'd role-play a Paris whore.

EDDIE: Wahey!

BEATRICE opens the door, EDDIE deliberately turns away.

BEATRICE: Faites entrer le jeune coq tout seul. Je saurai m'en occuper.

EDDIE: Go on my son!

PHILIP is ushered in by BEATRICE. EDDIE shuts the door. He has a little listen with ear against the door. Then he finds a DO NOT DISTURB sign and hangs it on the door handle. Then he goes over to the cupboard and opens the cupboard door. ANDRE has a glass of wine in his hand and a guilty look on his face as he sits there with headphones on. EDDIE tops up his glass and in exchange EDDIE takes the head phones from him and puts them on. He does this standing outside the cupboard. The story on his face tells the story of Bed 1. Enter NICOLA on the phone. EDDIE turns and sees her, keeping the headphones on – big double take.

During the next NICOLA looks around the room searching for her Blackberry.

NICOLA: (*On the phone.*) It's all the same complaints basically. Torture; criminalisation of dissent; honour killings – violence against women. Hang on Claude.

EDDIE: Hello love.

NICOLA: I left my Blackberry. Have you seen it?

EDDIE: Yer bramble?

NICOLA: It's a hand held computer.

EDDIE: Nothing hand held round here.

NICOLA: Sorry Claude… I've got some free time this afternoon now and I thought I might try and catch a meeting with Beatrice Renard, the Chair of the Women's Committee… She's a loony obviously, have you seen the Daily Mail today… God I know, talk about pouring petrol on the flames… I'll try and knock some sense into her. Ciao!

NICOLA finds the handcuffs. And picks them up with a heavy question mark.

EDDIE: Is that it love?

NICOLA is alerted by noises within Bed 1 and goes over and sees the DO NOT DISTURB sign. She then tries the door but it is locked. She goes over to EDDIE and takes the headphones off his head.

This is Andre, he's a kind of spook, anti-fraud squad.

EDDIE says nothing but the sounds of love-making come through the open speakers of the headphones. NICOLA opens the headphones up so they act like speakers. Enter SASHA.

SASHA: (*To EDDIE.*) What's she doing here?

EDDIE: That's worr I wanna know. You know this is Nicola don't yer?!

SASHA: Aghh!!!

SASHA backs off with a hand over her mouth. NICOLA leans into the cupboard and turns the volume up. They stand and listen to BEATRICE come to orgasm.

Silence.

The key in the lock of Bed 1 is heard to turn, and the door opens slowly. PHILIP stands there still bandaged fully, then he starts to unravel the bandages as he talks.

PHILIP: We've got champagne somewhere. Or do you want one of your spritzers? You know, I think that doctor's overreacted. I caught a bit of flash alright but I'm not wearing these bloody bandages. They itch!

BEATRICE appears in the doorway wearing a sheet. PHILIP is a little into the main room. He takes the pads of his eyes and looks across at EDDIE and NICOLA.

How did you get over there? Fully clothed?

Then he looks back at BEATRICE. It dawns on him. He does the double take again, and a then a third time.

Has anyone got a ciggie?

To black.

End of Act Two.

Act Three

One hour later. PHILIP sits on the sofa. He has the bowl of medicinal twiglets in front of him and is placing broken twiglets between his toes and powdering them. His eye bandages are flicked up on his forehead like sunglasses. He is half dressed ie: bare feet, vest and suit trousers held up by braces. His clothing is crumpled and in need of a wash and iron. EDDIE is half drunk and opening a bottle of wine. SASHA is ironing his shirts. The iced water glass is set in the fridge.

SASHA: Which shirt do you want to wear?

PHILIP: How do I know what to wear? I'm not gay.

SASHA: Oh come on! Frau Flugelhammerlein's coming round and you've still got twiglets between your toes.

PHILIP: I incredibly do not give a damn.

SASHA: Everyone's impressed by the letter bomb.

EDDIE: Aye, all of a sudden you're flavour of the month.

SASHA: The man with his finger on the pulse of the Turkey issue.

EDDIE: You're a dead cert to get nominated for President. And if yer get to be President yer can let Turkey in the back door AND pick up yer nine million. Which is a lot of money even after yer've deducted my consultancy fees.

PHILIP: But I've lost Nicola! I'm forty-six and there's been a lot of women, and I'm not ashamed of that. I'm incredibly proud of it, actually, in a kind of immature adolescent sort of way. But she's the only woman I've ever loved. L O V E Deed, as opposed to just shagged a lot over an extended period of time. She's gone!

SASHA: (*Holding Blackberry.*) I've found her Blackberry. She'll come back for this.

EDDIE: And when she comes back – propose. Marriage. Get down on one knee and do the right thing.

PHILIP: Did you get down on one knee to propose Eddie?

EDDIE: I'd already been on me knees for twennie minutes. Worst case of carpet burns I'd ever had. (*To PHILIP.*) Stop sulking! Sitting there like a little lad with a broken toy.

PHILIP: It's not broken. Damn! I wish I understood women. I went to boarding school where Club International Magazine was our only source of information. I've still not recovered from the disappointment of realising that women don't wear shoes in bed.

EDDIE: (*Laughing through the speech.*) Yer've accidentally fucked the wrong woman, it's easily done. At least you haven't married the wrong woman like most of the rest of humanity.

SASHA: Did you marry the wrong woman Eddie?

EDDIE: I married the right woman. Me and our lass started when we was sixteen. Mind you she's always been a frisky one. You only had to sneeze twice and she had twins.

PHILIP: – Too much information Eddie!

EDDIE: The hysterectomy's med her worse. She blames the operation. She ses all it did was convert the workshop into a playroom.

PHILIP: (*Covering his ears.*) – I'm not listening!

EDDIE: Even with the change –

PHILIP: Shut up!

EDDIE: Mind you it's tekken me forty years to find out what our lass really wants in bed.

PHILIP: And what does she want in bed?

EDDIE: George Clooney. My generation in't the problem, it's you youngsters. All this women's rights merlarkey.

SASHA: – Oh!!

EDDIE: – No, no, don't get me wrong, I'm a bit of a 'new man' mesen, it's quite right that our women have careers, work, but that means they have kids much later, or not at all, whereas yer Muslins are bang at it – knocking 'em out –

SASHA: Eddie!

EDDIE: Mark my words, hundred years time Europe'll be Eurabia, unrecognisable, and then!? Well, yer gays, yer Jews –

Enter ANDRE from the cupboard interrupting.

ANDRE: – Messieurs Dames.

EDDIE: Did you get your evidence then son?

PHILIP: What did Renard say when we were in bed?

ANDRE: (*Reading, from note book.*) 'Encore, encore, non, à gauche, voilà! oh, oh, mon dieu, mon dieu, oui, oui, oui, ooooohhh!

PHILIP: That's not gonna stand up in a court is it?

ANDRE: 'owever, when she was alone in the room she rang her father who it seems is on his death bed as we speak. Her father is Yves Renard, I do not know of him but he sounds like a rich man.

PHILIP: He is Mr Monsieur Bricolage.

ANDRE: Then he is a very wealthy man indeed. Madame Renard is his eldest child and should inherit the fortune but the father has stipulated that she will get nothing unless she marries before he dies.

PHILIP: But she's already married!

ANDRE: D'accord! And that is what interests me. OLAF have done some investigation. Jean-Claude Renard, her supposed husband, lives in the Dordogne.

PHILIP: Why? Is he English?

ANDRE: There are still some French people left in the Dordogne.

SASHA: But she's the MEP for Strasbourg.

ANDRE: Her husband is a tobacco farmer with eighty-three hectares of land. Each year he receives two hundred thousand euros from the Common Agricultural Policy.

EDDIE: Last year I fraudulently claimed sixty thousand quid's worth of set-aside.

PHILIP: What – for land you were still farming?

EDDIE: For the A64 to Scarborough. I give the money back. On'y did it to prove me point.

ANDRE: And what exactly is your point?

EDDIE: That you're all fucking idiots.

ANDRE: To prove that she is not married to this Jean-Claude we will have to squeeze more information out of her.

PHILIP: I've done enough squeezing for one day.

ANDRE: I 'ave 'ad an idea. It came to me in ze cupboard. When she comes back from her interview with the gendarme, I would like you to ask her to marry you.

PHILIP: What?!

EDDIE: If she agrees to marry you, that proves that she is single.

ANDRE: And confirms that the tobacco farm is a sophisticated criminal fraud.

PHILIP: Fantastic for you, you've only got to catch her, I've got to fucking marry her and run an imaginary tobacco farm!

SASHA: Which doesn't exist.

PHILIP: Running an imaginary tobacco farm won't be as bad as running a real tobacco farm, but I'm an MEP for God's sake and the prospect of work of any sort has given me an imaginary bad back!

ANDRE: Just propose to her. If she says yes that will be the end of it, I will have my catch.

PHILIP: I'm sorry, this is a sensationally bad idea and I'm not having anything to do with it.

ANDRE: You forget, I now have solid evidence of your misuse of the expenses budget, particularly in relation to the employment of Miss Nicola Daws who, in her own words, earns eighty thousand euros a year for doing 'bugger all'. And I can 'ave Sasha 'ere deported back to M–

PHILIP puts his hand over ANDRE's mouth.

PHILIP: – Don't say the M word!

EDDIE: What you're really saying is you've got him over a barrel?

ANDRE: I do not understand.

EDDIE: You've got him over a fifty litre non-elliptical container generally used for the transportation or storage of wet goods.

ANDRE: Exactement!

EDDIE: What's the M word?

PHILIP: Murmansk.

SASHA paces the room smashing things.

SASHA: Govnik! Manda! Zhopa! Khuyesos!

PHILIP: Alright, I'll do it. But remember the deal is you don't arrest her before tomorrow and the vote in the Parliament.

ANDRE: D'accord!

ANDRE goes back into the cupboard; the door slams. Main doors open and NICOLA comes in. She's obviously been shopping and is carrying a plastic carrier bag with DOCTOR LOVE on it, and a brown briefcase the same as MEHMET's and EDDIE's. This latter new case she puts on SASHA's desk (or on the floor, or anywhere that feels right – but it has to end up on SASHA's desk).

NICOLA: Did you have sex with that woman in there?

PHILIP: Define sex.

NICOLA: Did you have full penetrative sex?

PHILIP: Define full penetrative sex.

NICOLA: Did you put your erect penis inside her vagina and orgasm?

PHILIP: Oh! I see what you mean! Yes.

NICOLA: This is for you.

She produces a box, not gift wrapped, and puts it on the coffee table.

The shop assistant said it was the perfect gift for a 'wanker'.

PHILIP: Really, you shouldn't have. A card would have been enough.

NICOLA exits to Bed 2.

That went quite well.

EDDIE: At least you're talking.

SASHA: 'Doctor Love'. That's that sex shop on the island, isn't it?

EDDIE: Aye, I'm banned from there.

PHILIP: What for?

EDDIE: Fighting.

PHILIP has opened the box and taken out a silicone female hand with painted nails and a rubber sucker on the base. He reads from the box.

PHILIP: The Helping Hand.

EDDIE: (*Reading from the box.*) 'This textured silicone hand has been moulded from a beautiful model to give you the not-so-solo-sex-sensation of a lifetime.

PHILIP sticks it to the coffee table using the rubber sucker, and sets it going on a slow speed.

'The variable speed stroke facility allows for slow sensual arousal or rapid satisfaction.' Warning: highly flammable.

(*Standing.*) Where's that dildo gone?

Enter NICOLA with Blackberry in hand. The men cower.

NICOLA: Sasha, since I now have some free time, I would like to meet with the Turkish Ambassador.

PHILIP: Why do you want to see Mehmet?

NICOLA: As the Secretary General of Human Rights Now! I'd like to discuss Article 301 of the Turkish Penal Code.

PHILIP: Nicola, please keep your work separate from my work. Do you really think now is the time –

NICOLA: – now is the time for making babies but when I turned up for that meeting you'd started without me!

NICOLA goes back into Bed 2.

PHILIP: Bugger! It's revenge. She's trying to fuck up my deal with the Turks.

EDDIE attaches the Helping Hand to a door upstage at about groin height. Then he takes the vibrator and puts it in the Helping Hand, standing next to it as if it were his own penis.

EDDIE: Oh I gerr it!

Enter the GENDARME. He sees EDDIE. He watches EDDIE.

Don't bother knocking then!

GENDARME: I am nearly concluding ze deep probing wiz Madame Renard. Ensuite, I have a need of Monsieur Mehmet Aziz.

SASHA: I've called him half an hour ago and he's on his way.

GENDARME: Zank you. May I remind you zat no one is to leave zis chambre wizout my permissions.

(*To EDDIE.*) You must be careful wiz zese rubber 'ands monsieur, zey are highly inflammable…apparently. Please, continue.

Exit GENDARME. EDDIE sits, leaving the vibrator in the Helping Hand stuck on the door.

PHILIP: Nicola thinks I'm a complete wanker. She hates me.

EDDIE: This is nowt! Yer know they really hate yer when yer gerr a paper shredder for Christmas.

SASHA: She loves you! You love her! Ask her to marry you and if she loves you then she may forgive you. It was an honest mistake.

PHILIP: But she'll think that I only want to marry her because it'll help with my nomination for President.

SASHA: Why would she think that?

PHILIP: Because she's incredibly perceptive. Alright! I'll ask her.

SASHA: Yes!

SASHA kisses PHILIP.

PHILIP: Nip out and buy a simple gold band. Save the receipt, I'll put it on expenses.

SASHA heads for the exit doors.

EDDIE: (*To SASHA.*) More booze an' all. Sash!

PHILIP: Champagne. Yes! And ciggies.

EDDIE: Don't get any cheap muck.

SASHA: (*In the doorway.*) I'll do all of those things for you, if one of you boys will get rid of a certain glass of water in the fridge. There's no further use for it, and I'm not touching it. OK?!

PHILIP: (*Stands.*) Stop! Renard, she might be pregnant!

EDDIE: Aye, mebbe a swimmer got through.

PHILIP: Sasha, we're going to need a morning after pill.

SASHA: You can't just buy morning after pills. There's a form to fill in and everything.

PHILIP: Fill the form in then!

SASHA: I'm not doing that, it's –

PHILIP: – Murmansk!

SASHA leaves with an angry slam of the door.

I just wanted a nice quiet day with Nicola.

EDDIE: Everything's going well. Yer've got Beatrice to recruit an 'undred Christian Democrats to vote for the censure –

PHILIP: – Ninety-seven.

EDDIE: – you've pretty much secured the Presidency, and that means nine million euros off the Turks and yer've had a shag, and that alone meks it a good day in my book. All we need now is for you to ask the lass yer love to marry yer.

Knock at the door. PHILIP leaps up and grabs his clothes off the ironing board and elsewhere.

PHILIP: Bugger! That'll be Frau Flugelhammerlein!

ANDRE opens the cupboard door.

ANDRE: You will be safe in ze cupboard with me!

PHILIP: Great!

(*To EDDIE.*) Can you amuse her for a minute? Don't upset her Eddie, please.

PHILIP goes into the cupboard, closing the door behind him. The Helping Hand is still stuck on the outside of the cupboard door. EDDIE opens the main doors once PHILIP is in the cupboard.

FRAU: (*Striding in.*) Guten tag!

EDDIE: Norr exactly a beautiful language is it, German? Ever been to Lille International railway station?

FRAU: Ja! Selbsverstandlich!

EDDIE: Yer waiting fer the Eurostar and yer always get the fost announcement in English: 'Attention please, attention please the next train for Brussels will be arriving at platform three in two minutes.' Then next, yer French: 'Attention si'il vous plaît, attention s'il vous plaît, le prochain train pour Brussels…' whatever. And then yer get yer German: 'ACHTUNG! ACHTUNG! DER NAECHSTE ZUG…!!!!' I nearly shit mesen.

PHILIP slowly opens the cupboard door and puts a hand round the door feeling for the Helping Hand. He gets the vibrator which he puts in his jacket pocket. Then he picks the Helping Hand off the door.

FRAU: Who are you?

EDDIE: Eddie Fredericks UK Independence Party.

FRAU: Wo ist Philip?!

EDDIE: He's putting a tie on. Do you want a drink?

FRAU: Water please. Train stations remind me of my grandfather. He was murdered in the camp at Dachau.

EDDIE: Jewish eh?

FRAU: Communist.

EDDIE: Just a different kind of fascism.

FRAU: He worked against the Nazis. He had a vision for Europe, the kind of vision you backward thinking independence parties hate. He dreamt of a continent of peoples living peacefully together, trading, enjoying each other's cultures and all working together –

EDDIE: – to rip off the English.

FRAU: He understood that the kind of blind, stupid nationalism, which you Europhobes so love, has created the wars that have blighted this continent. You, your party of little Englanders – you're ridiculous, you have no policies, you have no leader, you have no principles.

During the next EDDIE starts preparing a clean glass of water with ice.

EDDIE: I'm democratically elected love, unlike the Commissioners. I feel sorry for them Eastern Europeans. Soon they'll realise that they've swapped dictatorship from Moscow for dictatorship from Brussels, Jo Stalin for Peter Mandelson. Stalin was a fascist and a mass murderer, but at least he weren't a poof.

FRAU: Homophobic too! Like everyone in your ridiculous party you're a myopic, small minded, racist moron –

EDDIE has prepared the drink and is about to offer the glass of clean water to FRAU FLUGELHAMMERLEIN.

EDDIE: – You can't upset me love.

FRAU: – and you smell of pigs.

EDDIE freezes.

EDDIE: D'yer wanna reconsider that last remark?

FRAU: Viz you comes a distinct smell of pigs.

EDDIE goes over to the fridge and picks out the 'medicinal water' and offers it to FRAU FLUGELHAMMERLEIN. She takes it. PHILIP has surreptitiously opened the cupboard door and, unseen, is watching the scene.

EDDIE: Cheers!

EDDIE clinks glasses, though FRAU FLUGELHAMMERLEIN doesn't want to. EDDIE drinks. FRAU FLUGELHAMMERLEIN raises the glass and drinks. EDDIE picks up the 'medicinal twiglets' and offers the bowl to FRAU FLUGELHAMMERLEIN.

Twiglet?

FRAU FLUGELHAMMERLEIN eats a twiglet. PHILIP comes out of the cupboard, fully dressed but looking dishevelled.

FRAU: Why have you come just out of the cupboard?

PHILIP: I…er…go in there to…do my Tai Chi.

FRAU: In a cupboard?

PHILIP: 'Cupboard Tai Chi'. It's like 'Travel Scrabble'. It's the perfect activity for people who like Tai Chi but don't like being watched. Is that water alright?

FRAU: Fine. Cold, and just a hint of salt.

FRAU drinks again.

PHILIP: And the twiglets?

FRAU: Excellent, I didn't know they did cheese flavoured.

PHILIP: Are they cheesy?

FRAU: Try one. Go on.

FRAU takes the bowl of twiglets from EDDIE and pushes it towards PHILIP. PHILIP balks at the offer.

Come on! I value your opinion. When you're President, which looks very likely, you'll need to form opinions on everything on the spur of the moment!

PHILIP eventually takes one and eats it.

PHILIP: (*With a full mouth of twiglet.*) There's a hint of brie.

FRAU: Correct! Now, everything's going fantastically well Philip.

PHILIP: Is it?

FRAU: Jawohl! The Christian Democrats are split in two! Their left wing is blaming their loony right wing for the jiffy bag bomb. We socialists will soon be running the Parliament and in a position to welcome Turkey into the EU. A secular democratic Muslim nation will act as a buffer to the fundamentalism of the terrorists.

PHILIP: So by accidentally having sex with the wrong woman, I've saved Europe from the Taliban?

FRAU: Essentially, yes! And you will be President! If you marry!

PHILIP: I'm going to propose to someone today.

FRAU FLUGELHAMMERLEIN puts an arm around PHILIP.

FRAU: I am not going to mutter you, but I had no children of my own. The choice of bride is important Phil. Imagine dinner with Bush, Putin, Bono. It's vital to have someone who's not going to show you up.

Enter NICOLA from Bed 2.

NICOLA: I'm going to fuck the next man who walks through this door.

PHILIP: Nicola! Darling! This is Frau Flugelhammerlein, my boss, the Socialist whip.

She closes the door.

FRAU: You're marrying a tart?

PHILIP: Her!? No, No!!

FRAU: You called her 'Nicola darling'.

PHILIP: That's her name – 'Nicola Darling'. She's Alistair Darling's mother.

EDDIE: Niece.

PHILIP: Yes! Niece!

FRAU: The President of the European Parliament needs a mature woman; sophisticated; charming; elegant and if she's a linguist, I can't tell you what a bonus that is.

Enter BEATRICE, through the main doors, looking elegant, wearing the blonde wig. EDDIE holds the door to Bed 2 closed so that NICOLA can't come out.

BEATRICE: Guten Tag, Frau Flugelhammerlein. Wie geht's?

FRAU: Es geht mir gut, danke. Und Sie?

BEATRICE: Prima! Vielen dank! Das Wetter hier in Strasbourg ist so warm.

FRAU: (*Shaking hands.*) Enchanté. (*To PHILIP.*) Your partner reminds me just a little of that Beatrice Renard who runs the Women's Committee?

PHILIP: My what?

FRAU: (*To BEATRICE.*) You're like an attractive, not mad version. (*Laughs.*)

BEATRICE: (*Laughs.*) L'habit ne fait pas le moine! À la prochaine.

BEATRICE goes into Bed 1.

FRAU: (*To PHILIP.*) She speaks French too. Fantastisch! Now she is the perfect wife for a President!

PHILIP: Isn't she!

FRAU: You two getting married is the best news I've had all day! (*To PHILIP.*) Brilliant work Philip!

FRAU FLUGELHAMMERLEIN makes to go. Enter SASHA quickly with a plastic shopping bag with wine bottles rattling and a brown briefcase. She doesn't notice FRAU FLUGELHAMMERLEIN.

PHILIP: Apart from letting Turkey in, as President, what are my other policies, what do I stand for?

FRAU: Anti-corruption, anti-excess, family values.

SASHA empties the bags.

SASHA: Booze, fags, morning after pills.

FRAU: Auf Wiedersehen.

EDDIE: Tarra!

FRAU FLUGELHAMMERLEIN exits. PHILIP slams the doors closed and leans back against them for support. PHILIP goes to the cupboard, opens it. ANDRE is revealed with headphones on.

PHILIP: (*To ANDRE.*) Are you ready to record this, because I'm only going to propose once OK!

ANDRE: On y va!

PHILIP closes the cupboard door. He goes over to SASHA's desk.

PHILIP: (*To SASHA.*) And give me one of those morning after pills. Eddie, get me a drink of water. Clean, fresh water please.

SASHA gives him a morning after pill and EDDIE begins preparing the glass. PHILIP knocks on Bed 1 door. BEATRICE opens it.

Will you marry me? Come on make your bloody mind up!

BEATRICE: Do you love me?

PHILIP: Of course I bloody love you! My heart aches when you're around.

BEATRICE: Not around, surely.

PHILIP: Eh?

BEATRICE: Say something romantic Philip!

PHILIP: Right. Er...compared to your beauty, roses are a bit shit. Well!? What is it?! Oui ou non!?

BEATRICE: Oh yes! Let's get married!

ANDRE: (*Off.*) Whooo!

BEATRICE: I think there is someone in the cupboard.

BEATRICE starts to move towards the cupboard. PHILIP grabs her.

PHILIP: We'll have plenty of time for looking in cupboards after we're married. Now, let me kiss you.

PHILIP is seen to put the morning after pill on the tip of his tongue. They begin a long, deep tongue kiss. NICOLA opens the door to Bed 2 and watches, unseen. She then returns to Bed 2 closing the door quietly. PHILIP slaps the back of his head and spits the morning after pill into BEATRICE's mouth. BEATRICE begins to choke. EDDIE is there with the drink.

Agh! I've lost a tooth!

BEATRICE: (*Choking.*) I'm choking!

PHIL: Here, take a drink, swallow.

BEATRICE drinks and swallows and heads for the door...

SASHA: Madame! You can't leave, the gendarme needs everyone to stay in this room.

BEATRICE: Gendarme?! Phuh! I have to see someone much more important. Philip, cheri, you have made me so happy.

She kisses PHILIP and leaves. PHILIP opens the cupboard door.

PHILIP: Did you get that?!

ANDRE: Oui! My fish is off ze hook and in ze pan!

NICOLA comes out of Bed 2. PHILIP slams the door of the cupboard.

NICOLA: Who is that woman? The one you were kissing?

PHILIP: That was incredibly not a kiss actually. It's an emergency medical procedure. A kissectomy. I learned it in the brownies.

NICOLA: I've seen pornography that was easier to watch!

PHILIP: It wasn't even a tonguey!

NICOLA: You were licking her kidneys!

NICOLA searches SASHA's desk for a pair of scissors.

Sasha, I'm looking for scissors.

PHILIP: (*Backing off.*) Nicola, will you marry me? What happened earlier, in there, was an accident.

NICOLA: Did you enjoy yourself during the accident?

PHILIP: Yes. But only because I thought it was you!

NICOLA: Tut!

PHILIP: You're the only woman I've ever really loved. And I mean LOVE. I'm not just talking about good sex.

EDDIE: Oh dear.

PHILIP: What?

NICOLA finds scissors without SASHA's help and advances on PHILIP. PHILIP instinctively shields his groin.

NICOLA: Asking me to marry you is a desperate attempt to win me back and you don't really mean it.

PHILIP: I do do mean it.

NICOLA cuts his tie in half, then his braces which results in his trousers falling down. Enter MEHMET through the main doors.

EDDIE: Oh bloody hell.

PHILIP pulls his trousers up. EDDIE pours himself another drink.

PHILIP: Mehmet?!

NICOLA: Mehmet Aziz?

MEHMET: Yes?

NICOLA: It's very good of you to meet me at such short notice. I'm Nicola Daws.

NICOLA offers her hand. MEHMET refuses it.

MEHMET: And the very worst enemy of the Turkish nation.

(*To PHILIP.*) You are lovers? With this woman?

PHILIP: (*Shaking his head as if to say No.*) Yes.

NICOLA: Please, sit down Mr Aziz.

During the next SASHA switches EDDIE's case for PHILIP's.

In order to make Turkey pass for a civilised society you've rushed through these harmonisation laws, but they are a veil, if I might use that word, and human rights abuses against women, political prisoners, writers –

PHILIP: – Mehmet, can I get you a drink?

MEHMET: (*To PHILIP.*) No!

Turkey is a modern secular democracy with exemplary standards.

NICOLA: Try telling that to Mr Hrant Dink.

MEHMET: We did not kill Mr Dink, it was some boy, some idiot.

NICOLA: You charged him under article 301 of the penal code with insulting Turkey. Why didn't you just stick a target on his chest!

PHILIP: Nibbles? We've got some clean twiglets.

MEHMET: No thank you!

NICOLA: You made him wide open to any Islamist nutter with a gun.

MEHMET: What do you expect if you go around saying that Turkey killed a million Armenian Christians!

NICOLA: So you admit that it is not possible to speak the truth in Turkey?

MEHMET: It is not the truth!

NICOLA: Your Nobel Prize winning author, Orhan Pamuk, has had to flee to America in fear of his life.

MEHMET: Reading his books anyone would think that Turkey is swarming with Taliban style executioners, and that it snows all the time!

NICOLA: Turkey only wants to join the EU for the grants. Money you desperately need to pay off the Turkish debt mountain.

MEHMET stands. Everyone stands and looks around for armed mullahs.

PHILIP: Shhh! You're not allowed to say Turkish debt mountain!

NICOLA: Article 301 does not apply to me, I'm not Turkish.

MEHMET: (*To PHILIP, standing.*) No! As an employee of Turkey you're not allowed to say Turkish debt mountain.

EDDIE: (*To MEHMET.*) That's twice today you've said Turkish debt mountain.

MEHMET: I would never say Turkish debt mountain, because that would be an insult to Turkishness which is a very serious crime for a Turk, and I might get my thumbs crushed.

NICOLA: So you admit that torture is prevalent in Turkey?

MEHMET: No! Turkey is perfect! Wherever Turks live together there is paradise! Have you never been to Stoke Newington?

MEHMET picks up EDDIE's case.

Our deal is off Mr Wardrobe!

PHILIP: What?!

MEHMET: I will take my briefcase back now!

PHILIP: Oh no please! It's a lovely case and I've bought shoes to match.

Enter GENDARME.

GENDARME: Ah voila! Monsieur Aziz. Please arrive quickly zis way for ze deep probe up ze rear passage.

MEHMET: Goodbye!

GENDARME and MEHMET leave, closing the doors behind them.

NICOLA: What was in that case?

SASHA has opened the remaining case. NICOLA can't see the contents.

SASHA: Ham sandwiches.

PHILIP: Yes!!!

EDDIE: Eh?

NICOLA: I don't understand.

SASHA stashes the money case in the cupboard.

PHILIP: Mr. Erdogan was impressed with my consultancy work for Turkey on the accession talks last December and as a thank you he gave me some ham sandwiches. Enough for a picnic.

NICOLA: Do I have a big neon sign on my head that says Gullible Fuckwit? What's in that case there?

PHILIP: (*Ashamed.*) One million euros.

NICOLA: Ah! Money. I can never compete with that can I? The next person I want to see –

PHILIP: – Will you marry me? I love you. (*To SASHA.*) Ring! (*Showing the band.*) Look! It's ninety-one carat gold.

NICOLA takes the band and turns it upside down.

NICOLA: Sixteen.

PHILIP: To get something as classy as that in England –

NICOLA: – you'd have to go to Argos. Some people can't be bought Phil.

She gives the ring back. NICOLA goes into Bed 2 and closes the door behind her.

PHILIP: (*To SASHA.*) How come we've still got the money?

SASHA: I switched briefcases.

PHILIP: You are the most incredibly gorgeous illegal Russian genius babe. I'm going to have to snog you.

SASHA presents her cheek for a peck, but PHILIP grabs her in a big squeeze. His trousers come down again. NICOLA opens the door to Bed 2 and watches. NICOLA waits.

NICOLA: (*To SASHA.*) Sasha, when you have a minute, please.

PHILIP: Agh!

PHILIP breaks off the snog and pulls his trousers up.

NICOLA: I'm having difficulty getting in touch with Madame Beatrice Renard, the Chair of the Women's Committee…

SASHA: She's had her mobile phone stolen.

NICOLA: That explains it then.

PHILIP: You don't want to see Beatrice – she's nuts.

NICOLA: And since when have you been an expert on mental illness? (*To SASHA.*) If you fix up a meeting that would be brilliant. My flight's at nine so I'll have to leave here by seven. (*To the room.*) If anyone has forgotten, I'm going to fuck – [the next man who comes through that door.]

PHILIP: – Yes, yes, we know.

NICOLA goes back into Bed 2. Enter BEATRICE through main doors. She is carrying some papers. EDDIE puts a chair up against NICOLA's door, ie Bed 2.

BEATRICE: Philip, my friend Roman is coming! He said he could do it!

PHILIP: Do what?

BEATRICE: Marry us. My father saved his life in the war. He was a Polish bomber pilot with the RAF.

PHILIP: Since when did Second World War Polish bomber pilots have the right to marry people?

BEATRICE: He's an Archbishop now. He's in the hotel for the conference! He'll be here in a minute. Mr Fredericks could you be a witness please?

EDDIE: Aye. And I'll be best man if yer want. I gorr a few jokes. This zebra walks into the farmyard –

SASHA: – wait! You can't get married just like that in France. The Lord Mayor has to perform a civil ceremony first.

BEATRICE produces a wad of papers. PHILIP snatches at them.

BEATRICE: The mayor of Strasbourg owes me seventy-three thousand euros and six favours. Today I cashed in the favours. You will see everything is in order.

Looking at the papers.

PHILIP: You've forged my signature!

BEATRICE: This way we can be married today!

Enter ANDRE from cupboard.

ANDRE: – Enough! Madame!

BEATRICE: Who are you?

ANDRE: You will find out who I am tomorrow.

BEATRICE: (*To PHILIP.*) I told you there was someone in the cupboard.

ANDRE: You are under arrest with OLAF, the fraud investigation team of the European Commission.

Enter the GENDARME carrying handcuffs. He doesn't fully enter the room at first and BEATRICE is obscured from his view by the open door of the room.

GENDARME: I have a need to arrest Madame Beatrice Renard.

BEATRICE opens the cupboard door and goes in.

Ze cell phone on the insides of the jiffy bag bom' was registered in her name. Now, say to me where she is?

PHILIP: The last time I saw her she was in here.

PHILIP ushers the GENDARME into Bed 1, and shuts the door behind him.

If she gets arrested before the vote tomorrow, I'll never be President!

ANDRE opens the cupboard door.

ANDRE: This woman is going to be my scalp, not his!

EDDIE: Yeah, you've put in the leg work kid.

ANDRE goes into the cupboard with BEATRICE. Enter GENDARME from Bed 1.

GENDARME: She is not in the insides zere. Why are you having a chair up 'ard against ze 'andle of zat chamber here?

PHILIP goes over to the door and blocks the GENDARME's path to the door.

PHILIP: Listen! You are in extreme danger of being shagged to death if you go in there.

GENDARME: Are you saying, zere is a woman inside zere who will force me to make love to her against my will?

PHILIP: That is incredibly bang on exactly what I'm saying officer. And you don't want that to happen do you, I can tell, you're a happily married man.

GENDARME: Step aside please.

PHILIP stands aside. The GENDARME moves the chair and opens the door, and looks in, he looks back, and is then yanked in by NICOLA. The door is slammed. There is screaming from the cupboard and BEATRICE falls out holding the Helping Hand.

BEATRICE: Ah!!! There are body parts in ze cupboard.

PHILIP takes the hand off of her.

PHILIP: Calm down! It's nothing unusual. It's a perfectly normal masturbating hand!

Knock at the door. SASHA opens it. Enter the ARCHBISHOP. During the next PHILIP is conscious of holding the masturbating hand. So he passes it to ANDRE, and slips on his jacket. ANDRE doesn't want it either so he passes it on to EDDIE, who doesn't want it, and who passes it on to SASHA who passes it back to PHILIP who secretes it up the sleeve of his jacket like a prosthetic limb.

BEATRICE: Roman! This is very kind of you.

ARCHBISHOP: (*Polish accent.*) I don't have long my Beatrice, I have to be in the plenary session in ten minutes.

BEATRICE kisses the ARCHBISHOP.

Bonjour. I am Archbishop Roman Borowczyk.

EDDIE: Ah, dziendobry.

ARCHBISHOP: Czy rozmawjasz Polsku?

EDDIE: Moy ojciec uciekl do Angli podczas wojny.
  Scarborough.

ARCHBISHOP: I am sorry we are being rude, speaking Polish.

PHILIP: (*To EDDIE.*) You speak Polish?

EDDIE: I'm half Polish. Me dad were a Jewish refugee.

BEATRICE: So you're a Jewish pig farmer?

EDDIE: No love. With yer Jews it's the mother's line in't it?

PHILIP: But you're not a proper hundred per cent
  Yorkshireman?

EDDIE: If it walks like a duck, and talks like a duck, it's a
  fucking duck.

ARCHBISHOP: Are you Mr Wardrobe?

PHILIP: Yes sir, hello.

*ARCHBISHOP offers his hand to shake. PHILIP thinks for a
moment and then shakes it with the Helping Hand because he
is holding his trousers up with his left hand.*

ARCHBISHOP: A prosthetic hand? My son, I sympathise. I
  have a false leg. I lost it in the war. How did you lose your
  hand?

PHILIP: Er…overuse. Too much of something.

Accidentally sets it to the rapid setting.

But this new hand is brilliant. Now I can do absolutely
everything I used to do before, only quicker.

ARCHBISHOP: Congratulations on your marriage! Can I see
  the civil licence please?

BEATRICE shoves the paperwork into his hands.

All in order! Now I'm a little expensive, four hundred euros an hour.

BEATRICE pays him a wad of cash which she produces from her suit.

NICOLA: (*Off.*) Ohagh!! Oh yes, yes, oh yes, don't stop, yes, Oh! Oh!

PHILIP listens at the door to Bed 2.

PHILIP: She's doing it. I didn't believe her. She's bloody well, incredibly doing it.

(*Sadly to the ARCHBISHOP.*) She's having it off with the gendarme!

PHILIP tries to open the door.

She's locked me out!

He tries to bash the door to Bed 2 down with his shoulder.

Stop, Nicola! Please! I love you!

ARCHBISHOP: Who is in there?

PHILIP: One of the bridesmaids.

ARCHBISHOP: You love one of the bridesmaids?

PHILIP: No! It's my mother.

EDDIE: Sister.

PHILIP: Yes, sister.

Enter GENDARME from Bed 2.

BEATRICE: Agh!

SASHA lifts the ARCHBISHOP's robes and BEATRICE hides in them. The ARCHBISHOP is shocked but is paid a bung by SASHA.

GENDARME: I have 'ad a good look. And I am now satisfied that Madame Renard is not within the insides.

EDDIE: Here you go son.

EDDIE gives the GENDARME a cigarette and lights it for him...

PHILIP: Did you make love to Nicola, the woman, my sister, within the inside? Did you!?

GENDARME: I am asking ze probing questions today, monsieur.

He takes a drag of the cigarette, and:

Now! Attempted murder wiz a jiffy bag bom' is a serious crime within the inside of France. I will find Madame Renard, arrest her, secure zis chambre, and then phone for back up.

SASHA: (*To GENDARME.*) Have you looked in the cupboard!?

The GENDARME gives PHILIP his cigarette, which PHILIP takes with the Helping Hand. SASHA opens the cupboard door and takes out the money case. The GENDARME goes into the cupboard. SASHA shuts the door on him. EDDIE holds the handle up so the GENDARME can't get out of the cupboard. Enter MEHMET through the main doors with briefcase.

MEHMET: Where is my money?!

EDDIE: Where are my bloody sandwiches?

MEHMET: (*Seeing the case on SASHA's desk.*) Aha!

He opens the case on SASHA's desk. He sees there's nothing in it. SASHA opens the door to Bed 1.

SASHA: I think your money is in here Mr Aziz!

MEHMET: Thank you, miss.

MEHMET goes into Bed 1 and SASHA jams a chair up against the handle. The cigarette has set light to the Helping Hand but PHILIP hasn't noticed. BEATRICE comes out from under the ARCHBISHOP's robes. There is banging on the cupboard door.

GENDARME: (*Off.*) Let me out!

BEATRICE: Cherie! This is our happy day!

PHILIP: Get off me! I'm going in there.

BEATRICE: Non! It is me you love! Come on!

*She tries to grab him and pull him over to the ARCHBISHOP but
she comes away with the hand which is on fire.*

Agh! Your wanking hand is on fire!

*BEATRICE throws it in the air and EDDIE catches it, thereby
leaving the cupboard door 'unlocked'. The GENDARME comes
out.*

EDDIE: Fire!

*SASHA throws the contents of the ice bucket at EDDIE holding
the hand. The contents miss the hand and hit the GENDARME
who loses his glasses on the floor. SASHA picks them up and
pockets them.*

GENDARME: Merde! Mes lunettes!

SASHA: Madame Renard is getting away!

SASHA opens one of the main doors and slams it.

She's escaping down the stairs!

*The GENDARME finds his own way uncertainly to the main doors
and goes through. SASHA slams the doors on him. ANDRE goes
back into the cupboard again. She then packs two of the cases
with A4 paper and dresses one of them on the top with notes.
The rest is then packed in her own case and left on the desk. She
takes the case with mainly paper and puts it in the fridge.*

(*Tapping her nose knowingly.*) I've switched the cases again,
the money is in the briefcase in the fridge, the other cases
are decoys!

BEATRICE: (*To ARCHBISHOP.*) Get on with it then!

ARCHBISHOP: Do we have two witnesses?

ANDRE: Oui! C'est moi!

ARCHBISHOP: (*To EDDIE.*) And you sir?

EDDIE: (*Drunk.*) Am I on? Alright! So this zebra walks into this farmyard, and ses to the chicken –

ARCHBISHOP: – Thank you! So, you are gathered here today to witness the joining in matrimony of –

PHILIP: (*To ARCHBISHOP.*) No, no, no, and incredibly not yet! Wait! There's only one woman I love, and there are no circumstances in which I would marry this woman today! No one living on this earth could persuade me that it is a good idea.

Enter FRAU FLUGELHAMMERLEIN.

FRAU: Congratulations Philip! Wunderbar!

PHILIP: What's wonderbar?

FRAU: You've got it! The Presidency! Conditional on you being married. And this woman is a perfect wife. (*To BEATRICE.*) Congratulations my dear.

PHILIP: All I've got to do is marry…this woman? And then I'm the most powerful man in Europe.

FRAU: Jawohl! Carry on Archbishop, sorry to interrupt.

ARCHBISHOP: (*To PHILIP.*) Do you have a ring?

PHILIP goes into his pocket searching for the ring and comes out with the vibrator which he sticks in his mouth and continues searching for the ring. He comes up with the ring.

PHILIP: (*Mumbled because of vibrator in mouth.*) Will this do?

ARCHBISHOP: Holy matrimony. Which is an honourable state of life instituted from the beginning by God himself, signifying to us the spiritual union –

SASHA: – No! I will not allow this to happen.

EDDIE: And the zebra ses to the chicken, 'What do you do here?'

There is banging on the door of Bed 1.

SASHA: (*To BEATRICE.*) Mehmet Aziz is in here, and I'm going to open the door.

BEATRICE: No! I will kill him!

SASHA: Or he'll kill you.

BEATRICE dives under the ARCHBISHOP's robes again. MEHMET comes out of Bed 1.

Beatrice Renard is hiding between the legs of this Archbishop.

MEHMET lifts the robes of the ARCHBISHOP to reveal BEATRICE.

MEHMET: You have insulted all of Turkish manhood!

BEATRICE: Ahhhh!!!!

During the next BEATRICE leaps up from between the ARCHBISHOP's legs holding his prosthetic leg which is now a weapon. She attacks MEHMET and lays him out. The ARCHBISHOP is hopping about the room until he finds something to lean against. ANDRE comes out of the cupboard and surreptitiously takes the briefcase from the fridge and goes back into the cupboard with it.

MEHMET: Agh!

ARCHBISHOP: Give me my leg back. I'm useless without it.

BEATRICE: You're useless with it!

SASHA: (*Indicating the cupboard.*) And the policeman who will arrest you is in here!

BEATRICE leaves, running with the ARCHBISHOP's leg.

ARCHBISHOP: Come back!

The ARCHBISHOP leaves, hopping. MEHMET is left on the floor groaning.

EDDIE: And the chicken ses, 'I shit everywhere, quack, and lay the odd egg.'

And the zebra ses to the pig, 'What do you do here?'

MEHMET gets up on his knees. SASHA shows him the briefcase dressed with money on the top and he takes it. SASHA helps him to his feet and out the door. Enter NICOLA from Bed 1. NICOLA and PHILIP face each other.

And the pig ses, 'I shit everywhere, oink a lot, and then when I'm fat enough they turn me into bacon.'

And the zebra ses to the horse, 'And what do you do here?' And the horse ses, 'Tek yer pyjamas off and I'll show yer.'

EDDIE slips down the wall totally drunk. SASHA comes into the room, having dumped MEHMET in the lift. She shuts the door behind her. There is a hiatus of silence.

PHILIP: (*To FRAU FLUGELHAMMERLEIN.*) I resign, as President.

FRAU: You can't do that, what about –

PHILIP: What's the point of anything, without kids. I want to be a dad. I don't want to be President.

FRAU: You have let down Europe, me, the party, socialism.

PHILIP: For the record. French – je suis désolé. German – ich entschuldige mich. English – I couldn't give a fuck. Now go, please! I have something important to say to this woman here. Get out!

FRAU FLUGELHAMMERLEIN leaves.

(*To NICOLA.*) I heard you in there. I forgive you. It's all my fault. I pushed you into it. It's me. I've only ever been any good at two things. Fucking up, and apologising. I know it's all over between us now. I guess it has to be. I've just gone that bit too far this time. Well, I want you to know that you're the only woman I've ever really loved. You're like a part of me. Ten years eh? Off and on. Always, no matter where I am or what I'm doing, and I've even known it when having dinner with another woman or even when I've been in bed with someone else, yeah, even then, whenever I think of you my heart leaps – you know like when you drive over a hump backed bridge, your heart, no not just your heart your guts leap upwards – well, that's always happened. Just the thought of you. I think that's how I know it's real. And I know that you think that there's only one love in my life – me. Well, you might be right, but I'm not whole without you, and I can't like myself without knowing that you're part of me and what I am, and in an incredibly not rational way the only reason I love me is because you love me, or I thought you did. Get Freud to chew on that one. Huh!

He looks sideways and sees SASHA standing there with the money case.

Money eh? I know what you're thinking. It doesn't interest me much. I've never had to work for it. Can you honestly think of a time when I was short of money. Me, a socialist. I don't understand it, that's the only intrigue with money.

He takes the case. Opens it, looks at it.

Has it ever made me happy?

He gives the money case back to SASHA.

Take it Sash, it's yours. Buy that house in the country for your parents. And thank you.

SASHA walks past him into Bed 2 and during the next collects her things. SASHA comes out of Bed 2.

SASHA: Thank you Phil. Thank you, thank you!

SASHA leaves.

NICOLA: I didn't do anything in there. With the gendarme.

PHILIP: You didn't?

NICOLA: No. I faked it.

PHILIP: You don't fake it with me do you?

NICOLA: No.

PHILIP: I wish you would.

NICOLA: Why?

PHILIP: It would make me feel better about myself.

He grabs her head, putting both hands over her ears. He is intense.

Will you marry me? Please!

NICOLA: Say that again.

PHILIP: Why?

NICOLA: I didn't hear you. You had your hands over my ears.

PHILIP: Will you marry me? Please.

NICOLA: Marry you? Why would I want to marry a sex-obsessed, self-obsessed –

PHILIP: I'm incredibly not self-obsessed. I sponsor a goat in Somalia.

NICOLA: And what's the goat called? Philip Wardrobe!

PHILIP: OK! OK! I want to marry you. I want to grow up.

NICOLA: It wouldn't work.

PHILIP: I'd make it work. I'd change.

NICOLA: People don't change. They stay the same and then they start to hate their partners who want them to change. Every day with you will be like this, alcohol, sex with strangers and athlete's foot. Marriage? I won't even vote for you again.

PHILIP: I want to go to the Cricketers on a Sunday afternoon with you as my wife.

NICOLA: Trophy wife now.

PHILIP: Walk there, hand in hand, over the fields, and have lunch, and you can leave me there, and pick me up later, like you usually do, and we can go to bed on a Sunday afternoon and have a Chinese take-away later on, and do those crispy duck pancakes thingies and watch some Jane Austen adaptation on telly which reinforces our love of England. Oh for fuck's sake Nicola!

PHILIP turns away.

NICOLA: Alright then.

PHILIP: What did you say?

NICOLA: Yes.

They kiss – long and complicated.

But I don't want to be Mrs Wardrobe.

They kiss.

PHILIP: We could go the double-barrelled route.

NICOLA: Wardrobe-Daws?

PHILIP: What's wrong with that?

NICOLA: It would be unfair on the kids. What are we going to do now?

Another kiss.

PHILIP: Right now, I'm going to make love to you so slowly and for so long, that in years to come it's gonna look like a gap in your CV.

They edge towards Bed 1 and go in without closing the door. A few moans of pleasure, a squeal. A moment later PHILIP comes out goes to the cupboard and opens it. We see ANDRE there with his headphones on. PHILIP takes his headphones off. ANDRE picks up his things. They shake hands and ANDRE leaves. Then PHILIP, with a lift in his step, heads for Bed 1, and before closing the door, has a brief, satisfied scan of the room, and closes the door.

To black.

The End.